COMMON SENSE

AND OTHER ESSAYS

Thomas Paine

CLASSY
PUBLISHING

COMMON SENSE AND OTHER ESSAYS
by Thomas Paine
Published by Classy Publishing, 2024

www.classypublishing.com
info@classypublishing.com

ISBN: 978-93-5522-537-5

Cover Image by memorystockphoto / Adobe Stock
Cover Design by Classy Publishing

CONTENTS

COMMON SENSE

Introduction

Perhaps the sentiments contained in the following pages, are not *yet* sufficiently fashionable to procure them general favor; a long habit of not thinking a thing *wrong*, gives it a superficial appearance of being *right*, and raises at first a formidable outcry in defense of custom. But the tumult soon subsides. Time makes more converts than reason.

As a long and violent abuse of power, is generally the Means of calling the right of it in question (and in matters too which might never have been thought of, had not the sufferers been aggravated into the inquiry) and as the King of England hath undertaken in his *own right*, to support the Parliament in what he calls *theirs*, and as the good people of this country are grievously oppressed by the combination, they have an undoubted privilege to inquire into the pretensions of both, and equally to reject the usurpation of *either*.

In the following sheets, the author hath studiously avoided everything which is personal among ourselves. Compliments as well as censure to individuals make no part thereof. The wise, and the worthy, need not the triumph of a pamphlet; and those whose sentiments are injudicious, or unfriendly, will cease of themselves unless too much pains are bestowed upon their conversion.

The cause of America is in a great measure the cause of all mankind. Many circumstances hath, and will arise, which are not local, but universal, and through which the principles of all lovers of mankind are affected, and in the event of which, their affections are interested. The laying a country desolate with fire and sword, declaring war against the natural rights of all mankind, and extirpating the defenders thereof from the face of the earth, is the concern of every man to whom nature hath given the power of feeling; of which class, regardless of party censure, is

THE AUTHOR

P.S. The publication of this new edition hath been delayed, with a view of taking notice (had it been necessary) of any attempt to refute the Doctrine of Independence. As no answer hath yet appeared, it is now presumed that none will, the time needful for getting such a performance ready for the public being considerably past.

Who the author of this production is, is wholly unnecessary to the public, as the object for attention is the *doctrine itself*, not the *man*. Yet it may not be unnecessary to say, that he is unconnected with any party, and under no sort of influence public or private, but the influence of reason and principle.

PHILADELPHIA, February 14, 1776

Of the Origin and Design of Government in General, with Concise Remarks on the English Constitution

Some writers have so confounded society with government, as to leave little or no distinction between them; whereas they are not only different, but have different origins. Society is produced by our wants, and government by our wickedness; the former promotes our happiness *positively* by uniting our affections, the latter *negatively* by restraining our vices. The one encourages intercourse, the other creates distinctions. The first a patron, the last a punisher.

Society in every state is a blessing, but government even in its best state is but a necessary evil; in its worst state an intolerable one; for when we suffer, or are exposed to the same miseries *by a government*, which we might expect in a country *without government*, our calamity is heightened by reflecting that we furnish the means by which we suffer. Government, like dress, is the badge of lost innocence; the palaces of kings are built on the ruins of the bowers of paradise. For were the impulses of conscience clear, uniform, and irresistibly obeyed, man would need no other lawgiver; but that not being the case, he finds it necessary to surrender up a part of his property to furnish means for the protection of the rest; and this he is induced to do by the same prudence which in every other case advises him out of two evils to choose the least. *Wherefore*, security being the true design and end of government, it unanswerably follows that whatever *form* thereof appears most likely to ensure it to us, with the least expense and greatest benefit, is preferable to all others.

In order to gain a clear and just idea of the design and end of government, let us suppose a small number of persons settled in some sequestered part of the earth, unconnected with the rest; they will then represent the first peopling of any country, or of the world. In this state of natural liberty, society will be their first thought. A thousand motives will excite them thereto, the strength of one man is so unequal to his wants, and his mind so unfitted for perpetual solitude, that he is soon obliged to seek assistance and relief of another, who in his turn requires the same. Four or five united would be able to raise a tolerable dwelling in the midst of a wilderness, but *one* man might labour out of the common period of life without accomplishing anything; when he had felled his timber he could not remove it, nor erect it after it was removed; hunger in the meantime would urge him from his work, and every different want call him a different way. Disease, nay even misfortune would be death, for though neither might be mortal, yet either would disable him from living, and reduce him to a state in which he might rather be said to perish than to die.

Thus necessity, like a gravitating power, would soon form our newly arrived emigrants into society, the reciprocal blessings of which, would supersede, and render the obligations of law and government unnecessary while they remained perfectly just to each other; but as nothing but heaven is impregnable to vice, it will unavoidably happen, that in proportion as they surmount the first difficulties of emigration, which bound them together in a common cause, they will begin to relax in their duty and attachment to each other; and this remissness, will point out the necessity of establishing some form of government to supply the defect of moral virtue.

Some convenient tree will afford them a Statehouse, under the branches of which, the whole colony may assemble to deliberate on public matters. It is more than probable that their first laws will have the title only of Regulations, and be enforced by no other penalty than public disesteem. In this first parliament every man, by natural right, will have a seat.

But as the colony increases, the public concerns will increase likewise, and the distance at which the members may be separated, will render it too inconvenient for all of them to meet on every occasion as at first, when their number was small, their habitations near, and the public concerns few and trifling. This will point out the convenience of their consenting to leave the legislative part to be managed by a select number chosen from the whole body, who are supposed to have the same concerns at stake which those who appointed them, and who will act in the same manner as the whole body would act were they present. If the colony continue increasing, it will become necessary to augment the number of the representatives, and that the interest of every part of the colony may be attended to, it will be found best to divide the whole into convenient parts, each part sending its proper number; and that the *elected* might never form to themselves an interest separate from the *electors*, prudence will point out the propriety of having elections often; because as the *elected* might by that means return and mix again with the general body of the *electors* in a few months, their fidelity to the public will be secured by the prudent reflection of not making a rod for themselves. And as this frequent interchange will establish a common interest with every part of the community, they will mutually and naturally support each other, and on this (not on the unmeaning name of king) depends the *strength of government, and the happiness of the governed.*

Here then is the origin and rise of government; namely, a mode rendered necessary by the inability of moral virtue to govern the world; here too is the design and end of government, viz. freedom and security. And however our eyes may be dazzled with show, or our ears deceived by sound; however prejudice may warp our wills, or interest darken our understanding, the simple voice of nature and of reason will say, it is right.

I draw my idea of the form of government from a principle in nature, which no art can overturn, viz. that the more simple anything is, the less liable it is to be disordered; and the easier repaired when disordered; and with this maxim in view, I offer a few remarks on the so much boasted constitution of England. That it was noble for the dark and slavish times in which it was erected, is granted. When the world was over run with tyranny the least remove therefrom was a glorious rescue. But that it is imperfect, subject to convulsions, and incapable of producing what it seems to promise, is easily demonstrated.

Absolute governments (though the disgrace of human nature) have this advantage with them, that they are simple; if the people suffer, they know the head from which their suffering springs; know likewise the remedy; and are not bewildered by a variety of causes and cures. But the constitution of England is so exceedingly complex, that the nation may suffer for years together without being able to discover in which part the fault lies; some will say in one and some in another, and every political physician will advise a different medicine.

I know it is difficult to get over local or long standing prejudices, yet if we will suffer ourselves to examine the component parts of the English constitution, we shall find them to be the base remains of two ancient tyrannies, compounded with some new republican materials.

First.—The remains of monarchical tyranny in the person of the King.

Secondly.—The remains of aristocratical tyranny in the persons of the Peers.

Thirdly.—The new republican materials, in the persons of the Commons, on whose virtue depends the freedom of England.

The two first, by being hereditary, are independent of the people; wherefore in a *constitutional sense* they contribute nothing towards the freedom of the state.

To say that the constitution of England is a *union* of three powers reciprocally *checking* each other, is farcical; either the words have no meaning, or they are flat contradictions.

To say that the Commons is a check upon the King, presupposes two things:

First.—That the King is not to be trusted without being looked after; or in other words, that a thirst for absolute power is the natural disease of monarchy.

Secondly.—That the Commons, by being appointed for that purpose, are either wiser or more worthy of confidence than the crown.

But as the same constitution which gives the Commons a power to check the King by withholding the supplies, gives afterwards the King a power to check the Commons, by empowering him to reject their other bills; it again supposes that the King is wiser than those whom it has already supposed to be wiser than him. A mere absurdity!

There is something exceedingly ridiculous in the composition of monarchy; it first excludes a man from the means of information, yet empowers him to act in cases where the highest judgment is required. The state of a king shuts him from the world, yet the business of a king requires him to know it thoroughly; wherefore the different parts, by unnaturally opposing and destroying each other, prove the whole character to be absurd and useless.

Some writers have explained the English constitution thus; the King, say they, is one, the people another; the Peers are a house in behalf of the King; the Commons in behalf of the people; but this hath all the distinctions of a house divided against itself; and though the expressions be pleasantly arranged, yet when examined they appear idle and ambiguous; and it will always happen, that the nicest construction that words are capable of, when applied to the description of some thing which either cannot exist, or is too incomprehensible to be within the compass of description, will be words of sound only, and though they may amuse the ear, they cannot inform the mind, for this explanation includes a previous question, viz. *how came the King by a power which the people are afraid to trust, and always obliged to check*? Such a power could not be the gift of a wise people, neither can any power, *which needs checking*, be from God; yet the provision, which the constitution makes, supposes such a power to exist.

But the provision is unequal to the task; the means either cannot or will not accomplish the end, and the whole affair is a felo de se; for as the greater weight will always carry up the less, and as all the wheels of a machine are put in motion by one, it only remains to know which power in the constitution has the most weight, for that will govern; and though the others, or a part of them, may clog, or, as the phrase is, check the rapidity of its motion, yet so long as they cannot stop it, their endeavors will be ineffectual: the first moving power will at last have its way, and what it wants in speed is supplied by time.

That the crown is this overbearing part in the English constitution needs not be mentioned, and that it derives its whole consequence merely from being the giver of places and pensions is self-evident; wherefore, though we have been wise enough to shut and lock a door against absolute monarchy, we at the same time have been foolish enough to put the Crown in possession of the key.

The prejudice of Englishmen, in favour of their own government by King, Lords and Commons, arises as much or more from national pride than reason. Individuals are undoubtedly safer in England than in some other countries, but the *will* of the King is as much the *law* of the land in Britain as in France, with this difference, that instead of proceeding directly from his mouth, it is handed to the people under the more formidable shape of an act of parliament. For the fate of Charles the First, hath only made kings more subtle—not more just.

Wherefore, laying aside all national pride and prejudice in favour of modes and forms, the plain truth is, that *it is wholly owing to the constitution of the people, and not to the constitution of the government* that the crown is not as oppressive in England as in Turkey.

An inquiry into the *constitutional errors* in the English form of government is at this time highly necessary; for as we are never in a proper condition of doing justice to others, while we continue under the influence of some leading partiality, so neither are we capable of doing it to ourselves while we remain fettered by any obstinate prejudice. And as a man who is attached to a prostitute is unfitted to choose or judge of a wife, so any prepossession in favour of a rotten constitution of government will disable us from discerning a good one.

Of Monarchy and Hereditary Succession

Mankind being originally equals in the order of creation, the equality could only be destroyed by some subsequent circumstance; the distinctions of rich and poor may in a great measure be accounted for, and that without having recourse to the harsh ill sounding names of oppression and avarice. Oppression is often the *consequence*, but seldom or never the *means* of riches; and though avarice will preserve a man from being necessitously poor, it generally makes him too timorous to be wealthy.

But there is another and greater distinction for which no truly natural or religious reason can be assigned, and that is, the distinction of men into Kings and Subjects. Male and female are the distinctions of nature, good and bad the distinctions of heaven; but how a race of men came into the world so exalted above the rest, and distinguished like some new species, is worth enquiring into, and whether they are the means of happiness or of misery to mankind.

In the early ages of the world, according to the scripture chronology, there were no kings; the consequence of which was there were no wars; it is the pride of kings which throw mankind into confusion. Holland without a king hath enjoyed more peace for this last century than any of the monarchial governments in Europe. Antiquity favors the same remark; for the quiet and rural lives of the first patriarchs hath a happy something in them, which vanishes away when we come to the history of Jewish royalty.

Government by kings was first introduced into the world by the Heathens, from whom the children of Israel copied the custom. It was the most prosperous invention the Devil ever set on foot for the promotion of idolatry. The Heathens paid divine honors to their deceased kings, and the christian world hath improved on the plan by doing the same to their living ones. How impious is the title of sacred majesty applied to a worm, who in the midst of his splendor is crumbling into dust!

As the exalting one man so greatly above the rest cannot be justified on the equal rights of nature, so neither can it be defended on the authority of scripture; for the will of the Almighty, as declared by Gideon and the prophet Samuel, expressly disapproves of government by kings. All anti-monarchical parts of scripture have been very smoothly glossed over in monarchical governments, but they undoubtedly merit the attention of countries which have their governments yet to form. "Render unto Caesar the things which are Caesar's" is the scripture doctrine of courts, yet it is no support of monarchical government, for the Jews at that time were without a king, and in a state of vassalage to the Romans.

Near three thousand years passed away from the Mosaic account of the creation, till the Jews under a national delusion requested a king. Till then their form of government (except in extraordinary cases, where the Almighty interposed) was a kind of republic administred by a judge and the elders of the tribes. Kings they had none, and it was held sinful to acknowledge any being under that title but the Lord of Hosts. And when a man seriously reflects on the idolatrous homage which is paid to the persons of kings, he need not wonder, that the Almighty, ever jealous of his honor, should disapprove of a form of government which so impiously invades the prerogative of heaven.

Monarchy is ranked in scripture as one of the sins of the Jews, for which a curse in reserve is denounced against them. The history of that transaction is worth attending to.

The children of Israel being oppressed by the Midianites, Gideon marched against them with a small army, and victory, thro' the divine interposition, decided in his favour. The Jews elate with success, and attributing it to the generalship of Gideon, proposed making him a king, saying, "Rule thou over us, thou and thy son and thy son's son." Here was temptation in its fullest extent; not a kingdom only, but an hereditary one, but Gideon in the piety of his soul replied, "I will not rule over you, neither shall my son rule over you. THE LORD SHALL RULE OVER YOU." Words need not be more explicit; Gideon doth not *decline* the honor, but denieth their right to give it; neither doth he compliment them with invented declarations of his thanks, but in the positive stile of a prophet charges them with disaffection to their proper Sovereign, the King of heaven.

About one hundred and thirty years after this, they fell again into the same error. The hankering which the Jews had for the idolatrous customs of the Heathens, is something exceedingly unaccountable; but so it was, that laying hold of the misconduct of Samuel's two sons, who were entrusted with some secular concerns, they came in an abrupt and clamorous manner to Samuel, saying, "Behold thou art old, and thy sons walk not in thy ways, now make us a king to judge us like all other nations." And here we cannot but observe that their motives were bad, viz. that they might be *like* unto other nations, i.e. the Heathens, whereas their true glory laid in being as much *unlike* them as possible. "But the thing displeased Samuel when they said, Give us a king to judge us; and Samuel prayed unto the Lord, and the Lord said unto Samuel, Hearken unto the voice of the people in all that they say unto thee, for they have not rejected thee, but they have rejected me, THAT I SHOULD NOT REIGN OVER THEM. According to all the works which they have done since the day that I brought them up out of Egypt, even unto this day; wherewith they have forsaken me and served other Gods; so do they also unto thee. Now therefore hearken unto their voice, howbeit, protest solemnly unto them and show them the manner of the king that shall reign over them," i.e. not of any particular king, but the general manner of the kings of the earth, whom Israel was so eagerly copying after. And notwithstanding the great distance of time and difference of manners, the character is still in fashion. "And Samuel told all the words of the Lord unto the people, that asked of him a king. And he said, This shall be the manner of the king that shall reign over you; he will take your sons and appoint them for himself, for his chariots, and to be his horsemen, and some shall run before his chariots" (this description agrees with the present mode of impressing men) "and he will appoint him captains over thousands and captains over fifties, and will set them to ear his ground and to reap his harvest, and to make his instruments of war, and instruments of his chariots; and he will take your daughters to be confectionaries, and to be cooks and to be bakers" (this describes the expense and luxury as well as the oppression of kings) "and he will take your fields and your olive yards, even the best of them, and give them to his servants; and he will take the tenth of your feed, and of your vineyards, and give them to his officers and to his servants" (by which we see that bribery, corruption and favoritism are the standing vices of kings) "and he will take the tenth of your men servants, and your maid servants, and your goodliest young men and your asses, and put them to his work; and he will take the tenth of your sheep, and ye shall be his servants, and ye shall cry out in that day because of your king which ye shall have chosen, AND THE LORD WILL NOT HEAR YOU IN THAT DAY." This accounts for the continuation of monarchy; neither do the characters of the few good kings which have lived since, either sanctify the title, or blot out the sinfulness of the origin; the high encomium given of David takes no notice of him *officially as a king*, but only as a *man* after God's own heart. "Nevertheless the People refused to obey the voice of Samuel, and they said, Nay, but we will have a king over us, that we may be like all the nations, and that our king may judge us, and go out before us, and fight our battles." Samuel continued to reason with them, but to no purpose; he set before them their ingratitude, but all would not avail; and seeing them fully bent on their folly, he cried out, "I will call unto the Lord, and he shall send thunder and rain" (which then was a punishment, being in the time of wheat harvest) "that ye may perceive and see that your wickedness is great which ye have done in the sight of the Lord, IN ASKING YOU A KING. So Samuel called unto the Lord, and the Lord sent thunder and rain that day, and all the people greatly feared the Lord and Samuel. And all the people said unto Samuel, Pray for thy servants unto the Lord thy God that we die not, for WE HAVE ADDED UNTO OUR SINS THIS EVIL, TO ASK A KING." These portions of scripture are direct and positive. They admit of no equivocal construction. That the Almighty hath here entered his protest against monarchical government is true, or the scripture is false. And a man hath good reason to believe that there is as much of kingcraft, as priestcraft, in withholding the scripture from the public in Popish countries. For monarchy in every instance is the Popery of government.

To the evil of monarchy we have added that of hereditary succession; and as the first is a degradation and lessening of ourselves, so the second, claimed as a matter of right, is an insult and an imposition on posterity. For all men being originally equals, no *one* by *birth* could have a right to set up his own family in perpetual preference to all others forever, and though himself might deserve *some* decent degree of honors of his cotemporaries, yet his descendants might be far too unworthy to inherit them. One of the strongest *natural* proofs of the folly of hereditary right in kings, is that nature disapproves it, otherwise she would not so frequently turn it into ridicule by giving mankind an *ass for a lion*.

Secondly, as no man at first could possess any other public honors than were bestowed upon him, so the givers of those honors could have no power to give away the right of posterity, and though they might say "We choose you for *our* head," they could not, without manifest injustice to their children, say "that your children and your children's children shall reign over *ours* forever." Because such an unwise, unjust, unnatural compact might (perhaps) in the next succession put them under the government of a rogue or a fool. Most wise men, in their private sentiments, have ever treated hereditary right with contempt; yet it is one of those evils, which when once established is not easily removed; many submit from fear, others from superstition, and the more powerful part shares with the king the plunder of the rest.

This is supposing the present race of kings in the world to have had an honorable origin: whereas it is more than probable, that, could we take off the dark covering of antiquity, and trace them to their first rise, that we should find the first of them nothing better than the principal ruffian of some restless gang, whose savage manners or preeminence in subtlety obtained him the title of chief among plunderers; and who by increasing in power, and extending his depredations, overawed the quiet and defenceless to purchase their safety by frequent contributions. Yet his electors could have no idea of giving hereditary right to his descendants, because such a perpetual exclusion of themselves was incompatible with the free and unrestrained principles they professed to live by. Wherefore, hereditary succession in the early ages of monarchy could not take place as a matter of claim, but as something casual or complimental; but as few or no records were extant in those days, and traditional history stuffed with fables, it was very easy, after the lapse of a few generations, to trump up some superstitious tale, conveniently timed, Muhammad-like, to cram hereditary right down the throats of the vulgar. Perhaps the disorders which threatened, or seemed to threaten, on the decease of a leader and the choice of a new one (for elections among ruffians could not be very orderly) induced many at first to favor hereditary pretensions; by which means it happened, as it hath happened since, that what at first was submitted to as a convenience, was afterwards claimed as a right.

England, since the conquest, hath known some few good monarchs, but groaned beneath a much larger number of bad ones; yet no man in his senses can say that their claim under William the Conqueror is a very honorable one. A French bastard landing with an armed banditti, and establishing himself king of England against the consent of the natives, is in plain terms a very paltry rascally original. It certainly hath no divinity in it. However, it is needless to spend much time in exposing the folly of hereditary right; if there are any so weak as to believe it, let them promiscuously worship the ass and lion, and welcome. I shall neither copy their humility, nor disturb their devotion.

Yet I should be glad to ask how they suppose kings came at first? The question admits but of three answers, viz. either by lot, by election, or by usurpation. If the first king was taken by lot, it establishes a precedent for the next, which excludes hereditary succession. Saul was by lot, yet the succession was not hereditary, neither does it appear from that transaction there was any intention it ever should. If the first king of any country was by election, that likewise establishes a precedent for the next; for to say, that the *right* of all future generations is taken away, by the act of the first electors, in their choice not only of a king, but of a family of kings forever, hath no parrallel in or out of scripture but the doctrine of original sin, which supposes the free will of all men lost in Adam; and from such comparison, and it will admit of no other, hereditary succession can derive no glory. For as in Adam all sinned, and as in the first electors all men obeyed; as in the one all mankind were subjected to Satan, and in the other to sovereignty; as our innocence was lost in the first, and our authority in the last; and as both disable us from reassuming some former state and privilege, it unanswerably follows that original sin and hereditary succession are parellels. Dishonorable rank! Inglorious connection! Yet the most subtle sophist cannot produce a juster simile.

As to usurpation, no man will be so hardy as to defend it; and that William the Conqueror was an usurper is a fact not to be contradicted. The plain truth is, that the antiquity of English monarchy will not bear looking into.

But it is not so much the absurdity as the evil of hereditary succession which concerns mankind. Did it ensure a race of good and wise men it would have the seal of divine authority, but as it opens a door to the *foolish*, the *wicked*, and the *improper*, it hath in it the nature of oppression. Men who look upon themselves born to reign, and others to obey, soon grow insolent; selected from the rest of mankind their minds are early poisoned by importance; and the world they act in differs so materially from the world at large, that they have but little opportunity of knowing its true interests, and when they succeed to the government are frequently the most ignorant and unfit of any throughout the dominions.

Another evil which attends hereditary succession is, that the throne is subject to be possessed by a minor at any age; all which time the regency, acting under the cover of a king, have every opportunity and inducement to betray their trust. The same national misfortune happens, when a king worn out with age and infirmity, enters the last stage of human weakness. In both these cases the public becomes a prey to every miscreant, who can tamper successfully with the follies either of age or infancy.

The most plausible plea, which hath ever been offered in favour of hereditary succession, is, that it preserves a nation from civil wars; and were this true, it would be weighty; whereas, it is the most barefaced falsity ever imposed upon mankind. The whole history of England disowns the fact. Thirty kings and two minors have reigned in that distracted kingdom since the conquest, in which time there have been (including the Revolution) no less than eight civil wars and nineteen rebellions. Wherefore instead of making for peace, it makes against it, and destroys the very foundation it seems to stand on.

The contest for monarchy and succession, between the houses of York and Lancaster, laid England in a scene of blood for many years. Twelve pitched battles, besides skirmishes and sieges, were fought between Henry and Edward. Twice was Henry prisoner to Edward, who in his turn was prisoner to Henry. And so uncertain is the fate of war and the temper of a nation, when nothing but personal matters are the ground of a quarrel, that Henry was taken in triumph from a prison to a palace, and Edward obliged to fly from a palace to a foreign land; yet, as sudden transitions of temper are seldom lasting, Henry in his turn was driven from the throne, and Edward recalled to succeed him. The parliament always following the strongest side.

This contest began in the reign of Henry the Sixth, and was not entirely extinguished till Henry the Seventh, in whom the families were united. Including a period of 67 years, viz. from 1422 to 1489.

In short, monarchy and succession have laid (not this or that kingdom only) but the world in blood and ashes. 'Tis a form of government which the word of God bears testimony against, and blood will attend it.

If we inquire into the business of a king, we shall find that in some countries they have none; and after sauntering away their lives without pleasure to themselves or advantage to the nation, withdraw from the scene, and leave their successors to tread the same idle round. In absolute monarchies the whole weight of business, civil and military, lies on the king; the children of Israel in their request for a king, urged this plea "that he may judge us, and go out before us and fight our battles." But in countries where he is neither a judge nor a general, as in England, a man would be puzzled to know what *is* his business.

The nearer any government approaches to a republic the less business there is for a king. It is somewhat difficult to find a proper name for the government of England. Sir William Meredith calls it a republic; but in its present state it is unworthy of the name, because the corrupt influence of the crown, by having all the places in its disposal, hath so effectually swallowed up the power, and eaten out the virtue of the House of Commons (the republican part in the constitution) that the government of England is nearly as monarchical as that of France or Spain. Men fall out with names without understanding them. For it is the republican and not the monarchical part of the constitution of England which Englishmen glory in, viz. the liberty of choosing a House of Commons from out of their own body—and it is easy to see that when republican virtue fails, slavery ensues. Why is the constitution of England sickly, but because monarchy hath poisoned the republic, the crown hath engrossed the Commons?

In England a king hath little more to do than to make war and give away places; which, in plain terms, is to impoverish the nation and set it together by the ears. A pretty business indeed for a man to be allowed eight hundred thousand sterling a year for, and worshipped into the bargain! Of more worth is one honest man to society and in the sight of God, than all the crowned ruffians that ever lived.

Thoughts on the Present State of American Affairs

In the following pages I offer nothing more than simple facts, plain arguments, and common sense; and have no other preliminaries to settle with the reader, than that he will divest himself of prejudice and prepossession, and suffer his reason and his feelings to determine for themselves; that he will put *on*, or rather that he will not put *off*, the true character of a man, and generously enlarge his views beyond the present day.

Volumes have been written on the subject of the struggle between England and America. Men of all ranks have embarked in the controversy, from different motives, and with various designs; but all have been ineffectual, and the period of debate is closed. Arms, as the last resource, decide the contest; the appeal was the choice of the King, and the continent hath accepted the challenge.

It hath been reported of the late Mr. Pelham (who though an able minister was not without his faults) that on his being attacked in the House of Commons on the score that his measures were only of a temporary kind, replied "they will last my time." Should a thought so fatal and unmanly possess the colonies in the present contest, the name of ancestors will be remembered by future generations with detestation.

The sun never shined on a cause of greater worth. 'Tis not the affair of a city, a country, a province, or a kingdom, but of a continent—of at least one eighth part of the habitable globe. 'Tis not the concern of a day, a year, or an age; posterity are virtually involved in the contest, and will be more or less affected, even to the end of time, by the proceedings now. Now is the seed time of continental union, faith and honor. The least fracture now will be like a name engraved with the point of a pin on the tender rind of a young oak; the wound will enlarge with the tree, and posterity read it in full grown characters.

By referring the matter from argument to arms, a new era for politics is struck; a new method of thinking hath arisen. All plans, proposals, etc. prior to the nineteenth of April, i.e. to the commencement of hostilities,[1] are like the almanacs of the last year; which, though proper then, are superseded and useless now. Whatever was advanced by the advocates on either side of the question then, terminated in one and the same point, viz. a union with Great Britain; the only difference between the parties was the method of effecting it; the one proposing force, the other friendship; but it hath so far happened that the first hath failed, and the second hath withdrawn her influence.

As much hath been said of the advantages of reconciliation, which, like an agreeable dream, hath passed away and left us as we were, it is but right, that we should examine the contrary side of the argument, and inquire into some of the many material injuries which these colonies sustain, and always will sustain, by being connected with, and dependant on Great Britain. To examine that connection and dependance, on the principles of nature and common sense, to see what we have to trust to, if separated, and what we are to expect, if dependant.

I have heard it asserted by some, that as America hath flourished under her former connection with Great Britain, that the same connection is necessary towards her future happiness, and will always have the same effect. Nothing can be more fallacious than this kind of argument. We may as well assert that because a child has thrived upon milk, that it is never to have meat, or that the first twenty years of our lives is to become a precedent for the next twenty. But even this is admitting more than is true, for I answer roundly, that America would have flourished as much, and probably much more, had no European power had anything to do with her. The commerce, by which she hath enriched herself are the necessaries of life, and will always have a market while eating is the custom of Europe.

But she has protected us, say some. That she has engrossed us is true, and defended the continent at our expense as well as her own is

1 At Lexington, Massachusetts, 1775. —Conway

admitted, and she would have defended Turkey from the same motive, viz. the sake of trade and dominion.

Alas, we have been long led away by ancient prejudices, and made large sacrifices to superstition. We have boasted the protection of Great Britain, without considering, that her motive was *interest* not *attachment*; that she did not protect us from *our enemies* on *our account*, but from *her enemies* on *her own account*, from those who had no quarrel with us on any *other account*, and who will always be our enemies on the *same account*. Let Britain wave her pretensions to the continent, or the continent throw off the dependance, and we should be at peace with France and Spain were they at war with Britain. The miseries of Hanover last war ought to warn us against connections.

It has lately been asserted in parliament, that the colonies have no relation to each other but through the parent country, i.e. that Pennsylvania and the Jerseys, and so on for the rest, are sister colonies by the way of England; this is certainly a very roundabout way of proving relationship, but it is the nearest and only true way of proving enemyship, if I may so call it. France and Spain never were, nor perhaps ever will be our enemies as *Americans*, but as our being the *subjects of Great Britain*.

But Britain is the parent country, say some. Then the more shame upon her conduct. Even brutes do not devour their young, nor savages make war upon their families; wherefore the assertion, if true, turns to her reproach; but it happens not to be true, or only partly so, and the phrase *parent* or *mother country* hath been Jesuitically adopted by the King and his parasites, with a low papistical design of gaining an unfair bias on the credulous weakness of our minds. Europe, and not England, is the parent country of America. This new world hath been the asylum for the persecuted lovers of civil and religious liberty from *every part* of Europe. Hither have they fled, not from the tender embraces of the mother, but from the cruelty of the monster; and it is so far true of England, that the same tyranny which drove the first emigrants from home, pursues their descendants still.

In this extensive quarter of the globe, we forget the narrow limits of three hundred and sixty miles (the extent of England) and carry our friendship on a larger scale; we claim brotherhood with every European christian, and triumph in the generosity of the sentiment.

It is pleasant to observe by what regular gradations we surmount the force of local prejudice, as we enlarge our acquaintance with the world.

A man born in any town in England divided into parishes, will naturally associate most with his fellow parishioners (because their interests in many cases will be common) and distinguish him by the name of *neighbour*; if he meet him but a few miles from home, he drops the narrow idea of a street, and salutes him by the name of *townsman*; if he travel out of the county, and meet him in any other, he forgets the minor divisions of street and town, and calls him *countryman*, i.e. *county-man*; but if in their foreign excursions they should associate in France or any other part of *Europe*, their local remembrance would be enlarged into that of *Englishmen*. And by a just parity of reasoning, all Europeans meeting in America, or any other quarter of the globe, are *countrymen*; for England, Holland, Germany, or Sweden, when compared with the whole, stand in the same places on the larger scale, which the divisions of street, town, and county do on the smaller ones; distinctions too limited for continental minds. Not one third of the inhabitants, even of this province, are of English descent. Wherefore I reprobate the phrase of parent or mother country applied to England only, as being false, selfish, narrow and ungenerous.

But, admitting that we were all of English descent, what does it amount to? Nothing. Britain, being now an open enemy, extinguishes every other name and title: and to say that reconciliation is our duty, is truly farcical. The first king of England, of the present line (William the Conqueror) was a Frenchman, and half the peers of England are descendants from the same country; therefore, by the same method of reasoning, England ought to be governed by France.

Much hath been said of the united strength of Britain and the colonies, that in conjunction they might bid defiance to the world. But this is mere presumption; the fate of war is uncertain, neither do the expressions mean anything; for this continent would never suffer itself to be drained of inhabitants, to support the British arms in either Asia, Africa, or Europe.

Besides what have we to do with setting the world at defiance? Our plan is commerce, and that, well attended to, will secure us the peace and friendship of all Europe; because, it is the interest of all Europe to have America a *free port*. Her trade will always be a protection, and her barrenness of gold and silver secure her from invaders.

I challenge the warmest advocate for reconciliation to show a single advantage that this continent can reap, by being connected with Great

Britain. I repeat the challenge; not a single advantage is derived. Our corn will fetch its price in any market in Europe, and our imported goods must be paid for buy them where we will.

But the injuries and disadvantages we sustain by that connection, are without number; and our duty to mankind at large, as well as to ourselves, instruct us to renounce the alliance: because, any submission to, or dependance on Great Britain, tends directly to involve this continent in European wars and quarrels; and sets us at variance with nations, who would otherwise seek our friendship, and against whom, we have neither anger nor complaint. As Europe is our market for trade, we ought to form no partial connection with any part of it. It is the true interest of America to steer clear of European contentions, which she never can do, while by her dependence on Britain, she is made the makeweight in the scale of British politics.

Europe is too thickly planted with kingdoms to be long at peace, and whenever a war breaks out between England and any foreign power, the trade of America goes to ruin, *because of her connection with Britain.* The next war may not turn out like the last, and should it not, the advocates for reconciliation now will be wishing for separation then, because neutrality in that case would be a safer convoy than a man of war. Everything that is right or natural pleads for separation. The blood of the slain, the weeping voice of nature cries, 'TIS TIME TO PART. Even the distance at which the Almighty hath placed England and America is a strong and natural proof that the authority of the one over the other was never the design of Heaven. The time likewise at which the continent was discovered, adds weight to the argument, and the manner in which it was peopled increases the force of it. The reformation was preceded by the discovery of America, as if the Almighty graciously meant to open a sanctuary to the persecuted in future years, when home should afford neither friendship nor safety.

The authority of Great Britain over this continent, is a form of government, which sooner or later must have an end: and a serious mind can draw no true pleasure by looking forward, under the painful and positive conviction, that what he calls "the present constitution" is merely temporary. As parents, we can have no joy, knowing that *this government* is not sufficiently lasting to ensure anything which we may bequeath to posterity: And by a plain method of argument, as we are running the next generation into debt, we ought to do the work of it, otherwise we use them meanly and pitifully. In order to discover the line of our duty rightly, we should take our children in our hand, and fix our station a few years farther into life; that eminence will present a prospect, which a few present fears and prejudices conceal from our sight.

Though I would carefully avoid giving unnecessary offence, yet I am inclined to believe, that all those who espouse the doctrine of reconciliation, may be included within the following descriptions.

Interested men, who are not to be trusted; weak men, who *cannot* see; prejudiced men, who *will not* see; and a certain set of moderate men, who think better of the European world than it deserves; and this last class, by an ill-judged deliberation, will be the cause of more calamities to this continent, than all the other three.

It is the good fortune of many to live distant from the scene of sorrow; the evil is not sufficient brought to *their* doors to make *them* feel the precariousness with which all American property is possessed. But let our imaginations transport us for a few moments to Boston; that seat of wretchedness will teach us wisdom, and instruct us forever to renounce a power in whom we can have no trust. The inhabitants of that unfortunate city, who but a few months ago were in ease and affluence, have now no other alternative than to stay and starve, or turn out to beg. Endangered by the fire of their friends if they continue within the city, and plundered by the soldiery if they leave it. In their present condition they are prisoners without the hope of redemption, and in a general attack for their relief, they would be exposed to the fury of both armies.

Men of passive tempers look somewhat lightly over the offences of Britain, and, still hoping for the best, are apt to call out, "Come, come, we shall be friends again, for all this." But examine the passions and feelings of mankind: bring the doctrine of reconciliation to the touchstone of nature, and then tell me, whether you can hereafter love, honour, and faithfully serve the power that hath carried fire and sword into your land? If you cannot do all these, then are you only deceiving yourselves, and by your delay bringing ruin upon posterity. Your future connection with Britain, whom you can neither love nor honour, will be forced and unnatural, and being formed only on the plan of present convenience, will in a little time fall into a relapse more wretched than the first. But if you say, you can still pass the violations over, then I ask, Hath your house been burnt? Hath your property been destroyed before your face? Are your wife and children destitute of a bed to lie on, or bread to live on? Have you lost a parent or a child by their hands, and yourself the ruined and wretched survivor? If you have not, then are you not a judge of those who have. But if you have, and still can shake hands with the murderers, then are you unworthy of the name of husband, father, friend, or lover, and whatever may be your rank or title in life, you have the heart of a coward, and the spirit of a sycophant.

This is not inflaming or exaggerating matters, but trying them by those feelings and affections which nature justifies, and without which, we should be incapable of discharging the social duties of life, or enjoying the felicities of it. I mean not to exhibit horror for the purpose of provoking revenge, but to awaken us from fatal and unmanly slumbers, that we may pursue determinately some fixed object. It is not in the power of Britain or of Europe to conquer America, if she do not conquer herself by *delay* and *timidity*. The present winter is worth an age if rightly employed, but if lost or neglected, the whole continent will partake of the misfortune; and there is no punishment which that man will not deserve, be he who, or what, or where he will, that may be the means of sacrificing a season so precious and useful.

It is repugnant to reason, to the universal order of things to all examples from former ages, to suppose, that this continent can longer remain subject to any external power. The most sanguine in Britain does not think so. The utmost stretch of human wisdom cannot, at this time, compass a plan short of separation, which can promise the continent even a year's security. Reconciliation is *now* a fallacious dream. Nature hath deserted the connection, and Art cannot supply her place. For, as Milton wisely expresses, "never can true reconcilement grow where wounds of deadly hate have pierced so deep."

Every quiet method for peace hath been ineffectual. Our prayers have been rejected with disdain; and only tended to convince us that nothing flatters vanity or confirms obstinacy in Kings more than repeated petitioning—and nothing hath contributed more than that very measure to make the Kings of Europe absolute: Witness Denmark and Sweden. Wherefore, since nothing but blows will do, for God's sake, let us come to a final separation, and not leave the next generation to be cutting throats, under the violated unmeaning names of parent and child.

To say, they will never attempt it again is idle and visionary, we thought so at the repeal of the stamp act, yet a year or two undeceived us; as well may we suppose that nations, which have been once defeated, will never renew the quarrel.

As to government matters, it is not in the power of Britain to do this continent justice: the business of it will soon be too weighty, and intricate, to be managed with any tolerable degree of convenience, by a power so distant from us, and so very ignorant of us; for if they cannot conquer us, they cannot govern us. To be always running three or four thousand miles with a tale or a petition, waiting four or five months for an answer, which when obtained requires five or six more to explain it in, will in a few years be looked upon as folly and childishness. There was a time when it was proper, and there is a proper time for it to cease.

Small islands not capable of protecting themselves, are the proper objects for kingdoms to take under their care; but there is something very absurd, in supposing a continent to be perpetually governed by an island. In no instance hath nature made the satellite larger than its primary planet, and as England and America, with respect to each other, reverses the common order of nature, it is evident they belong to different systems: England to Europe, America to itself.

I am not induced by motives of pride, party, or resentment to espouse the doctrine of separation and independance; I am clearly, positively, and conscientiously persuaded that it is the true interest of this continent to be so; that everything short of *that* is mere patchwork, that it can afford no lasting felicity—that it is leaving the sword to our children, and shrinking back at a time, when, a little more, a little farther, would have rendered this continent the glory of the earth.

As Britain hath not manifested the least inclination towards a compromise, we may be assured that no terms can be obtained worthy the acceptance of the continent, or any ways equal to the expense of blood and treasure we have been already put to.

The object, contended for, ought always to bear some just proportion to the expense. The removal of North, or the whole detestable junto, is a matter unworthy the millions we have expended. A temporary stoppage of trade was an inconvenience, which would have sufficiently ballanced the repeal of all the acts complained of, had such repeals been obtained; but if the whole continent must take up arms, if every man must be a soldier, it is scarcely worth our while to fight against a contemptible ministry only. Dearly, dearly, do we pay for the repeal of the acts, if that is all we fight for; for in a just estimation, it is as great a folly to pay a

Bunker-hill price for law as for land. As I have always considered the independancy of this continent, as an event which sooner or later must arrive, so from the late rapid progress of the continent to maturity, the event could not be far off. Wherefore, on the breaking out of hostilities, it was not worth the while to have disputed a matter, which time would have finally redressed, unless we meant to be in earnest; otherwise, it is like wasting an estate on a suit at law, to regulate the trespasses of a tenant whose lease is just expiring. No man was a warmer wisher for reconciliation than myself, before the fatal nineteenth of April 1775, but the moment the event of that day was made known, I rejected the hardened, sullen tempered Pharaoh of England forever; and disdain the wretch, that with the pretended title of FATHER OF HIS PEOPLE can unfeelingly hear of their slaughter, and composedly sleep with their blood upon his soul.

But admitting that matters were now made up, what would be the event? I answer, the ruin of the continent. And that for several reasons.

First. The powers of governing still remaining in the hands of the king, he will have a negative over the whole legislation of this continent. And as he hath shown himself such an inveterate enemy to liberty, and discovered such a thirst for arbitrary power; is he, or is he not, a proper man to say to these colonies, "You shall make no laws but what I please." And is there any inhabitant in America so ignorant, as not to know, that according to what is called the *present constitution*, that this continent can make no laws but what the king gives leave to; and is there any man so unwise as not to see, that (considering what has happened) he will suffer no law to be made here, but such as suit *his* purpose. We may be as effectually enslaved by the want of laws in America, as by submitting to laws made for us in England. After matters are made up (as it is called) can there be any doubt, but the whole power of the crown will be exerted, to keep this continent as low and humble as possible? Instead of going forward we shall go backward, or be perpetually quarrelling or ridiculously petitioning. We are already greater than the king wishes us to be, and will he not hereafter endeavour to make us less? To bring the matter to one point. Is the power who is jealous of our prosperity, a proper power to govern us? Whoever says *No* to this question is an *independant*, for independancy means no more than this, whether we shall make our own laws, or whether the King, the greatest enemy this continent hath, or can have, shall tell us "there shall be no laws but such as I like."

But the King you will say has a negative in England; the people there can make no laws without his consent. In point of right and good order, there is something very ridiculous, that a youth of twenty-one (which hath often happened) shall say to several millions of people, older and wiser than himself, I forbid this or that act of yours to be law. But in this place I decline this sort of reply, though I will never cease to expose the absurdity of it, and only answer that England being the King's residence, and America not so, makes quite another case. The King's negative *here* is ten times more dangerous and fatal than it can be in England; for *there* he will scarcely refuse his consent to a bill for putting England into as strong a state of defence as possible, and in America he would never suffer such a bill to be passed.

America is only a secondary object in the system of British politics, England consults the good of *this* country, no farther than it answers her *own* purpose. Wherefore, her own interest leads her to suppress the growth of *ours* in every case which doth not promote her advantage, or in the least interferes with it. A pretty state we should soon be in under such a secondhand government, considering what has happened! Men do not change from enemies to friends by the alteration of a name: And in order to show that reconciliation *now* is a dangerous doctrine, I affirm, *that it would be policy in the king at this time, to repeal the acts for the sake of reinstating himself in the government of the provinces;* in order that HE MAY ACCOMPLISH BY CRAFT AND SUBTLETY, IN THE LONG RUN, WHAT HE CANNOT DO BY FORCE AND VIOLENCE IN THE SHORT ONE. Reconciliation and ruin are nearly related.

Secondly. That as even the best terms, which we can expect to obtain, can amount to no more than a temporary expedient, or a kind of government by guardianship, which can last no longer than till the colonies come of age, so the general face and state of things, in the interim, will be unsettled and unpromising. Emigrants of property will not choose to come to a country whose form of government hangs but by a thread, and who is every day tottering on the brink of commotion and disturbance; and numbers of the present inhabitants would lay hold of the interval, to dispense of their effects, and quit the continent.

But the most powerful of all arguments is, that nothing but independance, i.e. a continental form of government, can keep the peace of the continent and preserve it inviolate from civil wars. I dread the event of a reconciliation with Britain now, as it is more than probable, that it will be followed by a revolt somewhere or other, the consequences of which may be far more fatal than all the malice of Britain.

Thousands are already ruined by British barbarity; (thousands more will probably suffer the same fate.) Those men have other feelings than us who have nothing suffered. All they *now* possess is liberty, what they before enjoyed is sacrificed to its service, and having nothing more to lose, they disdain submission. Besides, the general temper of the colonies, towards a British government, will be like that of a youth who is nearly out of his time; they will care very little about her. And a government which cannot preserve the peace is no government at all, and in that case we pay our money for nothing; and pray what is it that Britain can do, whose power will be wholly on paper, should a civil tumult break out the very day after reconciliation? I have heard some men say, many of whom I believe spoke without thinking, that they dreaded an independance, fearing that it would produce civil wars. It is but seldom that our first thoughts are truly correct, and that is the case here; for there are ten times more to dread from a patched up connection than from independance. I make the sufferers case my own, and I protest, that were I driven from house and home, my property destroyed, and my circumstances ruined, that as man, sensible of injuries, I could never relish the doctrine of reconciliation, or consider myself bound thereby.

The colonies have manifested such a spirit of good order and obedience to continental government, as is sufficient to make every reasonable person easy and happy on that head. No man can assign the least pretence for his fears, on any other grounds, than such as are truly childish and ridiculous, viz. that one colony will be striving for superiority over another.

Where there are no distinctions there can be no superiority, perfect equality affords no temptation. The republics of Europe are all (and we may say always) in peace. Holland and Switzerland are without wars, foreign or domestic: Monarchical governments, it is true, are never long at rest; the crown itself is a temptation to enterprising ruffians at *home*; and that degree of pride and insolence ever attendant on regal authority, swells into a rupture with foreign powers in instances where a republican government, by being formed on more natural principles, would negociate the mistake.

If there is any true cause of fear respecting independance, it is because no plan is yet laid down. Men do not see their way out. Wherefore, as an opening into that business, I offer the following hints; at the same time modestly affirming, that I have no other opinion of them myself, than that they may be the means of giving rise to something better. Could the straggling thoughts of individuals be collected, they would frequently form materials for wise and able men to improve into useful matter.

Let the assemblies be annual, with a President only. The representation more equal, their business wholly domestic, and subject to the authority of a Continental Congress.

Let each colony be divided into six, eight, or ten, convenient districts, each district to send a proper number of delegates to Congress, so that each colony send at least thirty. The whole number in Congress will be at least 390. Each Congress to sit and to choose a president by the following method. When the delegates are met, let a colony be taken from the whole thirteen colonies by lot, after which let the whole Congress choose (by ballot) a president from out of the delegates of *that* province. In the next Congress, let a colony be taken by lot from twelve only, omitting that colony from which the president was taken in the former Congress, and so proceeding on till the whole thirteen shall have had their proper rotation. And in order that nothing may pass into a law but what is satisfactorily just, not less than three fifths of the Congress to be called a majority. He that will promote discord, under a government so equally formed as this, would have joined Lucifer in his revolt.

But as there is a peculiar delicacy, from whom, or in what manner, this business must first arise, and as it seems most agreeable and consistent that it should come from some intermediate body between the governed and the governors, that is, between the Congress and the people, let a CONTINENTAL CONFERENCE be held, in the following manner, and for the following purpose.

A committee of twenty-six members of Congress, viz. two for each colony. Two members from each House of Assembly, or Provincial Convention; and five representatives of the people at large, to be chosen in the capital city or town of each province, for, and in behalf of the whole province, by as many qualified voters as shall think proper to attend from all parts of the province for that purpose; or, if more convenient, the representatives may be chosen in two or three of the most populous parts thereof. In this conference, thus assembled, will be united, the two grand principles of business, *knowledge* and *power*. The members of Congress, Assemblies, or Conventions, by having had experience in national concerns, will be able and useful counsellors, and the whole, being impowered by the people, will have a truly legal authority.

The conferring members being met, let their business be to frame a CONTINENTAL CHARTER, or Charter of the United Colonies; (answering to what is called the Magna Charta of England) fixing the number and manner of choosing members of Congress, members of Assembly, with their date of sitting, and drawing the line of business and jurisdiction between them: Always remembering, that our strength is continental, not provincial. Securing freedom and property to all men, and above all things, the free exercise of religion, according to the dictates of conscience; with such other matter as is necessary for a charter to contain. Immediately after which, the said Conference to dissolve, and the bodies which shall be chosen comformable to the said charter, to be the legislators and governors of this continent for the time being: Whose peace and happiness, may GOD preserve, AMEN.

Should anybody of men be hereafter delegated for this or some similar purpose, I offer them the following extracts from that wise observer on governments, Dragonetti. "The science," says he, "of the politician consists in fixing the true point of happiness and freedom. Those men would deserve the gratitude of ages, who should discover a mode of government that contained the greatest sum of individual happiness, with the least national expense." (Dragonetti on *Virtues and Rewards.*)

But where, say some, is the King of America? I'll tell you, friend, he reigns above, and doth not make havoc of mankind like the Royal Brute of Britain. Yet that we may not appear to be defective even in earthly honors, let a day be solemnly set apart for proclaiming the charter; let it be brought forth placed on the divine law, the word of God; let a crown be placed thereon, by which the world may know, that so far as we approve of monarchy, that in America THE LAW IS KING. For as in absolute governments the King is law, so in free countries the law *ought* to be King; and there ought to be no other. But lest any ill use should afterwards arise, let the crown at the conclusion of the ceremony be demolished, and scattered among the people whose right it is.

A government of our own is our natural right: and when a man seriously reflects on the precariousness of human affairs, he will become convinced, that it is infinitely wiser and safer, to form a constitution of our own in a cool deliberate manner, while we have it in our power, than to trust such an interesting event to time and chance. If we omit it now, some Massanello[2] may hereafter arise, who laying hold of popular disquietudes, may collect together the desperate and the discontented, and by assuming to themselves the powers of government, may sweep away the liberties of the continent like a deluge. Should the government of America return again into the hands of Britain, the tottering situation of things will be a temptation for some desperate adventurer to try his fortune; and in such a case, what relief can Britain give? Ere she could hear the news, the fatal business might be done; and ourselves suffering like the wretched Britons under the oppression of the Conqueror. Ye that oppose independance now, ye know not what ye do; ye are opening a door to eternal tyranny, by keeping vacant the seat of government. There are thousands, and tens of thousands, who would think it glorious to expel from the continent, that barbarous and hellish power, which hath stirred up the Indians and Negroes to destroy us; the cruelty hath a double guilt, it is dealing brutally by us, and treacherously by them.

To talk of friendship with those in whom our reason forbids us to have faith, and our affections wounded through a thousand pores instruct us to detest, is madness and folly. Every day wears out the little remains of kindred between us and them, and can there be any reason to hope, that as the relationship expires, the affection will increase, or that we shall agree better, when we have ten times more and greater concerns to quarrel over than ever?

Ye that tell us of harmony and reconciliation, can ye restore to us the time that is past? Can ye give to prostitution its former innocence? Neither can ye reconcile Britain and America. The last cord now is broken, the people of England are presenting addresses against us. There are injuries which nature cannot forgive; she would cease to be nature if she did. As well can the lover forgive the ravisher of his mistress, as the continent forgive the murders of Britain. The Almighty hath implanted in us these unextinguishable feelings for good and wise purposes. They are the guardians of his image in our hearts. They distinguish us from the herd of common animals. The social compact would dissolve, and

[2] Thomas Anello, otherwise Massanello, a fisherman of Naples, who after spiriting up his countrymen in the public market place, against the oppressions of the Spaniards, to whom the place was then subject, prompted them to revolt, and in the space of a day became King.

justice be extirpated the earth, or have only a casual existence were we callous to the touches of affection. The robber and the murderer would often escape unpunished, did not the injuries which our tempers sustain, provoke us into justice.

O! ye that love mankind! Ye that dare oppose, not only the tyranny, but the tyrant, stand forth! Every spot of the old world is overrun with oppression. Freedom hath been hunted round the globe. Asia, and Africa, have long expelled her. Europe regards her like a stranger, and England hath given her warning to depart. O! receive the fugitive, and prepare in time an asylum for mankind.

Of the Present Ability of America: With Some Miscellaneous Reflections

I have never met with a man, either in England or America, who hath not confessed his opinion, that a separation between the countries would take place one time or other: And there is no instance in which we have shown less judgment, than in endeavouring to describe, what we call, the ripeness or fitness of the Continent for independance.

As all men allow the measure, and vary only in their opinion of the time, let us, in order to remove mistakes, take a general survey of things, and endeavour, if possible, to find out the *very* time. But we need not go far, the inquiry ceases at once, for the *time hath found us.* The general concurrence, the glorious union of all things, proves the fact.

It is not in numbers, but in unity, that our great strength lies; yet our present numbers are sufficient to repel the force of all the world. The Continent hath, at this time, the largest body of armed and disciplined men of any power under Heaven; and is just arrived at that pitch of strength, in which no single colony is able to support itself, and the whole, when united, can accomplish the matter, and either more, or, less than this, might be fatal in its effects. Our land force is already sufficient, and as to naval affairs, we cannot be insensible, that Britain would never suffer an American man of war to be built, while the continent remained in her hands. Wherefore, we should be no forwarder an hundred years hence in that branch than we are now; but the truth is, we should be less so, because the timber of the country is every day diminishing, and that, which will remain at last, will be far off and difficult to procure.

Were the continent crowded with inhabitants, her sufferings under the present circumstances would be intolerable. The more sea port towns we had, the more should we have both to defend and to lose. Our present numbers are so happily proportioned to our wants, that no man need be idle. The diminution of trade affords an army, and the necessities of an army create a new trade.

Debts we have none; and whatever we may contract on this account will serve as a glorious memento of our virtue. Can we but leave posterity with a settled form of government, an independant constitution of its own, the purchase at any price will be cheap. But to expend millions for the sake of getting a few vile acts repealed, and routing the present ministry only, is unworthy the charge, and is using posterity with the utmost cruelty; because it is leaving them the great work to do, and a debt upon their backs, from which they derive no advantage. Such a thought is unworthy a man of honor, and is the true characteristic of a narrow heart and a pidling politician.

The debt we may contract doth not deserve our regard if the work be but accomplished. No nation ought to be without a debt. A national debt is a national bond; and when it bears no interest, is in no case a grievance. Britain is oppressed with a debt of upwards of one hundred and forty millions sterling, for which she pays upwards of four millions interest. And as a compensation for her debt, she has a large navy; America is without a debt, and without a navy; yet for the twentieth part of the English national debt, could have a navy as large again. The navy of England is not worth, at this time, more than three millions and an half sterling.

* * *

The first and second editions of this pamphlet were published without the following calculations, which are now given as a proof that the above estimation of the navy is just. See Entic's *Naval History*, Intro., page 56.

The charge of building a ship of each rate, and furnishing her with masts, yards, sails and rigging, together with a proportion of eight months boatswain's and carpenter's sea-stores, as calculated by Mr. Burchett, Secretary to the navy.

Number of guns	*Cost in £*
For a ship of 100 guns,	£35,553
90	29,886
80	23,638
70	17,785
60	14,197
50	10,606
40	7,558
30	5,846
20	3,710

And from hence it is easy to sum up the value, or cost rather, of the whole British navy, which in the year 1757, when it was at its greatest glory consisted of the following ships and guns:

Ships.	*Guns.*	*Cost of one (£).*	*Cost of all (£).*
6	100	35,553	213,318
12	90	29,886	358,632
12	80	23,638	283,656
43	70	17,785	764,755
35	60	14,197	496,895
40	50	10,606	424,240
45	40	7,558	340,110
58	20	3,710	215,180
85	Sloops, bombs and fireships, one with another, at	2,000	170,000
		Cost	3,266,786
		Remains for Guns	233,214
		Total	3,500,000

No country on the globe is so happily situated, or so internally capable of raising a fleet as America. Tar, timber, iron, and cordage are her natural produce. We need go abroad for nothing. Whereas the Dutch, who make large profits by hiring out their ships of war to the Spaniards and Portuguese, are obliged to import most of the materials they use. We ought to view the building a fleet as an article of commerce, it being the natural manufactory of this country. It is the best money we can lay out.

A navy when finished is worth more than it cost. And is that nice point in national policy, in which commerce and protection are united. Let us build; if we want them not, we can sell; and by that means replace our paper currency with ready gold and silver.

In point of manning a fleet, people in general run into great errors; it is not necessary that one fourth part should be sailors. The Terrible privateer, Captain Death, stood the hottest engagement of any ship last war, yet had not twenty sailors on board, though her complement of men was upwards of two hundred. A few able and social sailors will soon instruct a sufficient number of active landmen in the common work of a ship. Wherefore, we never can be more capable to begin on maritime matters than now, while our timber is standing, our fisheries blocked up, and our sailors and shipwrights out of employ. Men of war, of seventy and eighty guns were built forty years ago in New England, and why not the same now? Shipbuilding is America's greatest pride, and in which, she will in time excel the whole world. The great empires of the east are mostly inland, and consequently excluded from the possibility of rivalling her. Africa is in a state of barbarism; and no power in Europe, hath either such an extent of coast, or such an internal supply of materials. Where nature hath given the one, she has withheld the other; to America only hath she been liberal of both. The vast empire of Russia is almost shut out from the sea; wherefore, her boundless forests, her tar, iron, and cordage are only articles of commerce.

In point of safety, ought we to be without a fleet? We are not the little people now, which we were sixty years ago; at that time we might have trusted our property in the streets, or fields rather; and slept securely without locks or bolts to our doors or windows. The case now is altered, and our methods of defence ought to improve with our increase of property. A common pirate, twelve months ago, might have come up the Delaware, and laid the city of Philadelphia under instant contribution, for what sum he pleased; and the same might have happened to other places. Nay, any daring fellow, in a brig of fourteen or sixteen guns, might have robbed the whole Continent, and carried off half a million of money. These are circumstances which demand our attention, and point out the necessity of naval protection.

Some, perhaps, will say, that after we have made it up with Britain, she will protect us. Can we be so unwise as to mean, that she shall keep a navy in our harbours for that purpose? Common sense will tell us, that the power which hath endeavoured to subdue us, is of all others, the most improper to defend us. Conquest may be effected under the pretence of friendship; and ourselves, after a long and brave resistance, be at last cheated into slavery. And if her ships are not to be admitted into our harbours, I would ask, how is she to protect us? A navy three or four thousand miles off can be of little use, and on sudden emergencies, none at all. Wherefore, if we must hereafter protect ourselves, why not do it for ourselves? Why do it for another?

The English list of ships of war, is long and formidable, but not a tenth part of them are at any one time fit for service, numbers of them not in being; yet their names are pompously continued in the list, if only a plank be left of the ship: and not a fifth part of such as are fit for service, can be spared on any one station at one time. The East and West Indies, Mediterranean, Africa, and other parts over which Britain extends her claim, make large demands upon her navy. From a mixture of prejudice and inattention, we have contracted a false notion respecting the navy of England, and have talked as if we should have the whole of it to encounter at once, and for that reason, supposed, that we must have one as large; which not being instantly practicable, have been made use of by a set of disguised Tories to discourage our beginning thereon. Nothing can be farther from truth than this; for if America had only a twentieth part of the naval force of Britain, she would be by far an over match for her; because, as we neither have, nor claim any foreign dominion, our whole force would be employed on our own coast, where we should, in the long run, have two to one the advantage of those who had three or four thousand miles to sail over, before they could attack us, and the same distance to return in order to refit and recruit. And although Britain, by her fleet, hath a check over our trade to Europe, we have as large a one over her trade to the West Indies, which, by laying in the neighbourhood of the Continent, is entirely at its mercy.

Some method might be fallen on to keep up a naval force in time of peace, if we should not judge it necessary to support a constant navy. If premiums were to be given to merchants, to build and employ in their service ships mounted with twenty, thirty, forty or fifty guns, (the premiums to be in proportion to the loss of bulk to the merchants,) fifty or sixty of those ships, with a few guardships on constant duty, would keep up a sufficient navy, and that without burdening ourselves with the evil so loudly complained of in England, of suffering their fleet in time of peace to lie rotting in the docks. To unite the sinews of commerce and defense is sound policy; for when our strength and our riches play into each other's hand, we need fear no external enemy.

In almost every article of defense we abound. Hemp flourishes even to rankness, so that we need not want cordage. Our iron is superior to that of other countries. Our small arms equal to any in the world. Cannon we can cast at pleasure. Saltpetre and gunpowder we are every day producing. Our knowledge is hourly improving. Resolution is our inherent character, and courage hath never yet forsaken us. Wherefore, what is it that we want? Why is it that we hesitate? From Britain we can expect nothing but ruin. If she is once admitted to the government of America again, this Continent will not be worth living in. Jealousies will be always arising; insurrections will be constantly happening; and who will go forth to quell them? Who will venture his life to reduce his own countrymen to a foreign obedience? The difference between Pennsylvania and Connecticut, respecting some unlocated lands, shows the insignificance of a British government, and fully proves, that nothing but Continental authority can regulate Continental matters.

Another reason why the present time is preferable to all others, is, that the fewer our numbers are, the more land there is yet unoccupied, which instead of being lavished by the king on his worthless dependants, may be hereafter applied, not only to the discharge of the present debt, but to the constant support of government. No nation under heaven hath such an advantage as this.

The infant state of the Colonies, as it is called, so far from being against, is an argument in favour of independance. We are sufficiently numerous, and were we more so, we might be less united. It is a matter worthy of observation, that the more a country is peopled, the smaller their armies are. In military numbers, the ancients far exceeded the moderns: and the reason is evident. For trade being the consequence of population, men become too much absorbed thereby to attend to anything else. Commerce diminishes the spirit, both of patriotism and military defence. And history sufficiently informs us, that the bravest achievements were always accomplished in the nonage of a nation. With the increase of commerce, England hath lost its spirit. The city of London, notwithstanding its numbers, submits to continued insults with the patience of a coward. The more men have to lose, the less willing are they to venture. The rich are in general slaves to fear, and submit to courtly power with the trembling duplicity of a spaniel.

Youth is the seed time of good habits, as well in nations as in individuals. It might be difficult, if not impossible, to form the Continent into one government half a century hence. The vast variety of interests, occasioned by an increase of trade and population, would create confusion. Colony would be against colony. Each being able might scorn each other's assistance: and while the proud and foolish gloried in their little distinctions, the wise would lament, that the union had not been formed before. Wherefore the *present time* is the *true time* for establishing it. The intimacy which is contracted in infancy, and the friendship which is formed in misfortune, are, of all others, the most lasting and unalterable. Our present union is marked with both these characters: we are young, and we have been distressed; but our concord hath withstood our troubles, and fixes a memorable area for posterity to glory in.

The present time, likewise, is that peculiar time, which never happens to a nation but once, viz. the time of forming itself into a government. Most nations have let slip the opportunity, and by that means have been compelled to receive laws from their conquerors, instead of making laws for themselves. First, they had a king, and then a form of government; whereas, the articles or charter of government, should be formed first, and men delegated to execute them afterward: but from the errors of other nations, let us learn wisdom, and lay hold of the present opportunity—*to begin government at the right end.*

When William the Conqueror subdued England, he gave them law at the point of the sword; and until we consent, that the seat of government, in America, be legally and authoritatively occupied, we shall be in danger of having it filled by some fortunate ruffian, who may treat us in the same manner, and then, where will be our freedom? where our property?

As to religion, I hold it to be the indispensable duty of all government, to protect all conscientious professors thereof, and I know of no other business which government hath to do therewith. Let a man throw aside that narrowness of soul, that selfishness of principle, which the niggards of all professions are so unwilling to part with, and he will be at once delivered of his fears on that head. Suspicion is the companion of mean souls, and the bane of all good society. For myself, I fully and conscientiously believe, that it is the will of the Almighty, that there should be diversity of religious opinions among us: It affords a larger field for our Christian kindness. Were we all of one way of thinking, our religious dispositions would want matter for probation; and on this liberal principle, I look on the various denominations among us, to be like children of the same family, differing only, in what is called, their Christian names.

In a former page, I threw out a few thoughts on the propriety of a Continental Charter (for I only presume to offer hints, not plans) and in this place, I take the liberty of re-mentioning the subject, by observing, that a charter is to be understood as a bond of solemn obligation, which the whole enters into, to support the right of every separate part, whether of religion, personal freedom, or property. A firm bargain and a right reckoning make long friends.

In another former page I likewise mentioned the necessity of a large and equal representation; and there is no political matter which more deserves our attention. A small number of electors, or a small number of representatives, are equally dangerous. But if the number of the representatives be not only small, but unequal, the danger is increased. As an instance of this, I mention the following; when the Associators petition was before the House of Assembly of Pennsylvania; twenty-eight members only were present, all the Bucks county members, being eight, voted against it, and had seven of the Chester members done the same, this whole province had been governed by two counties only, and this danger it is always exposed to. The unwarrantable stretch likewise, which that house made in their last sitting, to gain an undue authority over the delegates of that province, ought to warn the people at large, how they trust power out of their own hands. A set of instructions for the Delegates were put together, which in point of sense and business would have dishonoured a schoolboy, and after being approved by a *few*, a *very few* without doors, were carried into the house, and there passed *in behalf of the whole colony*; whereas, did the whole colony know with what ill-will that house hath entered on some necessary public measures, they would not hesitate a moment to think them unworthy of such a trust.

Immediate necessity makes many things convenient, which if continued would grow into oppressions. Expedience and right are different things. When the calamities of America required a consultation, there was no method so ready, or at that time so proper, as to appoint persons from the several Houses of Assembly for that purpose; and the wisdom with which they have proceeded hath preserved this continent from ruin. But as it is more than probable that we shall never be without a CONGRESS, every well wisher to good order must own that the mode for choosing members of that body, deserves consideration. And I put it as a question to those, who make a study of mankind, whether *representation and election* is not too great a power for one and the same body of men to possess? When we are planning for posterity, we ought to remember that virtue is not hereditary.

It is from our enemies that we often gain excellent maxims, and are frequently surprised into reason by their mistakes. Mr. Cornwall (one of the Lords of the Treasury) treated the petition of the New York Assembly with contempt, because *that* house, he said, consisted but of twenty-six members, which trifling number, he argued, could not with decency be put for the whole. We thank him for his involuntary honesty.[3]

TO CONCLUDE, however strange it may appear to some, or however unwilling they may be to think so, matters not, but many strong and striking reasons may be given, to show, that nothing can settle our affairs so expeditiously as an open and determined declaration for independance. Some of which are,

First—It is the custom of nations, when any two are at war, for some other powers, not engaged in the quarrel, to step in as mediators, and bring about the preliminaries of a peace: but while America calls herself the Subject of Great Britain, no power, however well disposed she may be, can offer her mediation. Wherefore, in our present state we may quarrel on forever.

Secondly—It is unreasonable to suppose, that France or Spain will give us any kind of assistance, if we mean only, to make use of that assistance for the purpose of repairing the breach, and strengthening the connection between Britain and America; because, those powers would be sufferers by the consequences.

Thirdly—While we profess ourselves the subjects of Britain, we must, in the eye of foreign nations, be considered as rebels. The precedent is somewhat dangerous to *their peace*, for men to be in arms under the name of subjects; we, on the spot, can solve the paradox: but to unite

[3] Those who would fully understand of what great consequence a large and equal representation is to a state, should read Burgh's *Political Disquisitions*.

resistance and subjection, requires an idea much too refined for common understanding.

Fourthly—Were a manifesto to be published, and despatched to foreign Courts, setting forth the miseries we have endured, and the peaceable methods we have ineffectually used for redress; declaring, at the same time, that not being able, any longer, to live happily or safely under the cruel disposition of the British Court, we had been driven to the necessity of breaking off all connections with her; at the same time, assuring all such Courts of our peaceable disposition towards them, and of our desire of entering into trade with them: such a memorial would produce more good effects to this Continent, than if a ship were freighted with petitions to Britain.

Under our present denomination of British subjects, we can neither be received nor heard abroad: the custom of all Courts is against us, and will be so, until, by an independance, we take rank with other nations.

These proceedings may at first appear strange and difficult; but, like all other steps which we have already passed over, will in a little time become familiar and agreeable: and until an independance is declared, the Continent will feel itself like a man who continues putting off some unpleasant business from day to day, yet knows it must be done, hates to set about it, wishes it over, and is continually haunted with the thoughts of its necessity.

Appendix

Since the publication of the first edition of this pamphlet, or rather, on the same day on which it came out, the King's Speech made its appearance in this city. Had the spirit of prophecy directed the birth of this production, it could not have brought it forth, at a more seasonable juncture, or a more necessary time. The bloody mindedness of the one, show the necessity of pursuing the doctrine of the other. Men read by way of revenge. And the Speech, instead of terrifying, prepared a way for the manly principles of Independance.

Ceremony, and even silence, from whatever motive they may arise, have a hurtful tendency when they give the least degree of countenance to base and wicked performances; wherefore, if this maxim be admitted, it naturally follows, that the King's Speech, as being a piece of finished villainy, deserved, and still deserves, a general execration, both by the Congress and the people. Yet, as the domestic tranquillity of a nation, depends greatly, on the *chastity* of what may properly be called NATIONAL MANNERS, it is often better to pass some things over in silent disdain, than to make use of such new methods of dislike, as might introduce the least innovation, on that guardian of our peace and safety. And, perhaps, it is chiefly owing to this prudent delicacy, that the King's Speech hath not before now suffered a public execution. The Speech if it may be called one, is nothing better than a wilful audacious libel against the truth, the common good, and the existence of mankind; and is a formal and pompous method of offering up human sacrifices to the pride of tyrants. But this general massacre of mankind, is one of the privileges, and the certain consequence of Kings; for as nature knows them *not*, they know *not her*, and although they are beings of our *own* creating, they know not *us*, and are become the gods of their creators. The Speech hath one good quality, which is, that it is not calculated to deceive, neither can we, even if we would, be deceived by it. Brutality and tyranny appear on the face of it. It leaves us at no loss: And every line convinces, even in the moment of reading, that he who hunts the woods for prey, the naked and untutored Indian, is less a Savage than the King of Britain.

Sir John Dalrymple, the putative father of a whining Jesuitical piece, fallaciously called, *The Address of the People of England to the Inhabitants of America*, hath, perhaps, from a vain supposition, that the people *here* were to be frightened at the pomp and description of a king, given, (though very unwisely on his part) the real character of the present one: "But," says this writer, "if you are inclined to pay compliments to an administration, which we do not complain of," (meaning the Marquis of Rockingham's at the repeal of the Stamp Act) "it is very unfair in you to withhold them from that prince, *by whose* NOD ALONE *they were permitted to do anything*." This is toryism with a witness! Here is idolatry even without a mask: And he who can calmly hear, and digest such doctrine, hath forfeited his claim to rationality—an apostate from the order of manhood—and ought to be considered as one who hath not only given up the proper dignity of man, but sunk himself beneath the rank of animals, and contemptibly crawls through the world like a worm.

However, it matters very little now, what the king of England either says or does; he hath wickedly broken through every moral and human obligation, trampled nature and conscience beneath his feet; and by a steady and constitutional spirit of insolence and cruelty, procured for himself an universal hatred. It is *now* the interest of America to provide for herself. She hath already a large and young family, whom it is more her duty to take care of, than to be granting away her property, to support a power who is become a reproach to the names of men and christians—YE, whose office it is to watch over the morals of a nation, of whatsoever sect or denomination ye are of, as well as ye, who are more immediately the guardians of the public liberty, if ye wish to preserve your native country uncontaminated by European corruption, ye must in secret wish a separation. But leaving the moral part to private reflection, I shall chiefly confine my farther remarks to the following heads.

First. That it is the interest of America to be separated from Britain.

Secondly. Which is the easiest and most practicable plan, RECONCILIATION or INDEPENDENCE? with some occasional remarks.

In support of the first, I could, if I judged it proper, produce the opinion of some of the ablest and most experienced men on this continent; and whose sentiments, on that head, are not yet publicly known. It is in reality a self-evident position: for no nation in a state of foreign dependance, limited in its commerce, and cramped and fettered in its legislative powers, can ever arrive at any material eminence. America doth not yet know what opulence is; and although the progress which she hath made stands unparalleled in the history of other nations, it is but childhood, compared with what she would be capable of arriving at, had she, as she ought to have, the legislative powers in her own hands. England is, at this time, proudly coveting what would do her no good, were she to accomplish it; and the Continent hesitating on a matter, which will be her final ruin if neglected. It is the commerce and not the conquest of America by which England is to be benefited, and that would in a great measure continue, were the countries as independant of each other as France and Spain; because in many articles, neither can go to a better market. But it is the independance of this country of Britain or any other, which is now the main and only object worthy of contention, and which, like all other truths discovered by necessity, will appear clearer and stronger every day.

First. Because it will come to that one time or other.

Secondly. Because the longer it is delayed the harder it will be to accomplish.

I have frequently amused myself both in public and private companies, with silently remarking, the specious errors of those who speak without reflecting. And among the many which I have heard, the following seems the most general, viz. that had this rupture happened forty or fifty years hence, instead of *now*, the Continent would have been more able to have shaken off the dependance. To which I reply, that our military ability, *at this time*, arises from the experience gained in the last war, and which in forty or fifty years time, would have been totally extinct. The Continent, would not, by that time, have had a General, or even a military officer left; and we, or those who may succeed us, would have been as ignorant of martial matters as the ancient Indians: And this single position, closely attended to, will unanswerably prove, that the present time is preferable to all others. The argument turns thus—at the conclusion of the last war, we had experience, but wanted numbers; and forty or fifty years hence, we should have numbers, without experience;

wherefore, the proper point of time, must be some particular point between the two extremes, in which a sufficiency of the former remains, and a proper increase of the latter is obtained: And that point of time is the present time.

The reader will pardon this digression, as it does not properly come under the head I first set out with, and to which I again return by the following position, viz.

Should affairs be patched up with Britain, and she to remain the governing and sovereign power of America, (which, as matters are now circumstanced, is giving up the point entirely) we shall deprive ourselves of the very means of sinking the debt we have, or may contract. The value of the back lands which some of the provinces are clandestinely deprived of, by the unjust extension of the limits of Canada, valued only at five pounds sterling per hundred acres, amount to upwards of twenty-five millions, Pennsylvania currency; and the quit-rents at one penny sterling per acre, to two millions yearly.

It is by the sale of those lands that the debt may be sunk, without burden to any, and the quit-rent reserved thereon, will always lessen, and in time will wholly support the yearly expense of government. It matters not how long the debt is in paying, so that the lands when sold be applied to the discharge of it, and for the execution of which, the Congress for the time being, will be the continental trustees.

I proceed now to the second head, viz. Which is the easiest and most practicable plan, RECONCILIATION or INDEPENDANCE; with some occasional remarks.

He who takes nature for his guide is not easily beaten out of his argument, and on that ground, I answer generally—That independance being a single simple line, contained within ourselves; and reconciliation, a matter exceedingly perplexed and complicated, and in which, a treacherous capricious court is to interfere, gives the answer without a doubt.

The present state of America is truly alarming to every man who is capable of reflection. Without law, without government, without any other mode of power than what is founded on, and granted by courtesy. Held together by an unexampled concurrence of sentiment, which, is nevertheless subject to change, and which every secret enemy is endeavouring to dissolve. Our present condition, is, Legislation without law; wisdom without a plan; constitution without a name;

and, what is strangely astonishing, perfect Independance contending for dependance. The instance is without a precedent; the case never existed before; and who can tell what may be the event? The property of no man is secure in the present unbraced system of things. The mind of the multitude is left at random, and seeing no fixed object before them, they pursue such as fancy or opinion starts. Nothing is criminal; there is no such thing as treason; wherefore, everyone thinks himself at liberty to act as he pleases. The Tories dared not have assembled offensively, had they known that their lives, by that act, were forfeited to the laws of the state. A line of distinction should be drawn, between, English soldiers taken in battle, and inhabitants of America taken in arms. The first are prisoners, but the latter traitors. The one forfeits his liberty, the other his head.

Notwithstanding our wisdom, there is a visible feebleness in some of our proceedings which gives encouragement to dissensions. The Continental Belt is too loosely buckled. And if something is not done in time, it will be too late to do anything, and we shall fall into a state, in which, neither *Reconciliation* nor *Independance* will be practicable. The king and his worthless adherents are got at their old game of dividing the Continent, and there are not wanting among us Printers who will be busy in spreading specious falsehoods. The artful and hypocritical letter which appeared a few months ago in two of the New York papers, and likewise in two others, is an evidence that there are men who want either judgment or honesty.

It is easy getting into holes and corners and talking of reconciliation: But do such men seriously consider, how difficult the task is, and how dangerous it may prove, should the Continent divide thereon. Do they take within their view, all the various orders of men whose situation and circumstances, as well as their own, are to be considered therein. Do they put themselves in the place of the sufferer whose *all* is *already* gone, and of the soldier, who hath quitted *all* for the defence of his country. If their ill judged moderation be suited to their own private situations *only*, regardless of others, the event will convince them, that "they are reckoning without their host."

Put us, say some, on the footing we were on in the year 1763: To which I answer, the request is not *now* in the power of Britain to comply with, neither will she propose it; but if it were, and even should be granted, I ask, as a reasonable question, By what means is such a corrupt and faithless court to be kept to its engagements? Another parliament, nay, even the present, may hereafter repeal the obligation, on the pretence, of its being violently obtained, or unwisely granted; and in that case, Where is our redress? No going to law with nations; cannon are the barristers of crowns; and the sword, not of justice, but of war, decides the suit. To be on the footing of 1763, it is not sufficient, that the laws only be put on the same state, but, that our circumstances, likewise, be put on the same state; our burnt and destroyed towns repaired or built up, our private losses made good, our public debts (contracted for defence) discharged; otherwise, we shall be millions worse than we were at that enviable period. Such a request, had it been complied with a year ago, would have won the heart and soul of the Continent, but now it is too late. "The Rubicon is passed."

Besides, the taking up arms, merely to enforce the repeal of a pecuniary law, seems as unwarrantable by the divine law, and as repugnant to human feelings, as the taking up arms to enforce obedience thereto. The object, on either side, doth not justify the means; for the lives of men are too valuable to be cast away on such trifles. It is the violence which is done and threatened to our persons; the destruction of our property by an armed force; the invasion of our country by fire and sword, which conscientiously qualifies the use of arms: and the instant, in which such a mode of defence became necessary, all subjection to Britain ought to have ceased; and the independancy of America, should have been considered, as dating its era from, and published by, *the first musket that was fired against her*. This line is a line of consistency; neither drawn by caprice, nor extended by ambition; but produced by a chain of events, of which the colonies were not the authors.

I shall conclude these remarks, with the following timely and well intended hints. We ought to reflect, that there are three different ways, by which an independancy may hereafter be effected; and that *one* of those *three*, will one day or other, be the fate of America, viz. By the legal voice of the people in Congress; by a military power; or by a mob: It may not always happen that our soldiers are citizens, and the multitude a body of reasonable men; virtue, as I have already remarked, is not hereditary, neither is it perpetual. Should an independancy be brought about by the first of those means, we have every opportunity and every encouragement before us, to form the noblest purest constitution on the face of the earth. We have it in our power to begin the world over again.

A situation, similar to the present, hath not happened since the days of Noah until now. The birthday of a new world is at hand, and a race of men, perhaps as numerous as all Europe contains, are to receive their portion of freedom from the event of a few months. The reflection is awful, and in this point of view, how trifling, how ridiculous, do the little, paltry cavillings of a few weak or interested men appear, when weighed against the business of a world.

Should we neglect the present favorable and inviting period, and an independance be hereafter effected by any other means, we must charge the consequence to ourselves, or to those rather, whose narrow and prejudiced souls, are habitually opposing the measure, without either inquiring or reflecting. There are reasons to be given in support of independance, which men should rather privately think of, than be publicly told of. We ought not now to be debating whether we shall be independant or not, but, anxious to accomplish it on a firm, secure, and honorable basis, and uneasy rather that it is not yet began upon. Every day convinces us of its necessity. Even the Tories (if such beings yet remain among us) should, of all men, be the most solicitous to promote it; for, as the appointment of committees at first, protected them from popular rage, so, a wise and well established form of government, will be the only certain means of continuing it securely to them. *Wherefore*, if they have not virtue enough to be WHIGS, they ought to have prudence enough to wish for independance.

In short, Independance is the only BOND that can tye and keep us together. We shall then see our object, and our ears will be legally shut against the schemes of an intriguing, as well, as a cruel enemy. We shall then too, be on a proper footing to treat with Britain; for there is reason to conclude, that the pride of that court will be less hurt by treating with the American states for terms of peace, than with those, whom she denominates "rebellious subjects," for terms of accommodation. It is our delaying it that encourages her to hope for conquest, and our backwardness tends only to prolong the war. As we have, without any good effect therefrom, withheld our trade to obtain a redress of our grievances, let us *now* try the alternative, by *independantly* redressing them ourselves, and then offering to open the trade. The mercantile and reasonable part in England, will be still with us; because, peace *with* trade, is preferable to war *without* it. And if this offer be not accepted, other courts may be applied to.

On these grounds I rest the matter. And as no offer hath yet been made to refute the doctrine contained in the former editions of this pamphlet, it is a negative proof, that either the doctrine cannot be refuted, or, that the party in favour of it are too numerous to be opposed. WHEREFORE, instead of gazing at each other with suspicious or doubtful curiosity; let each of us, hold out to his neighbour the hearty hand of friendship, and unite in drawing a line, which, like an act of oblivion shall bury in forgetfulness every former dissension. Let the names of Whig and Tory be extinct; and let none other be heard among us, than those of *a good citizen, an open and resolute friend, and a virtuous supporter of the* RIGHTS *of* MANKIND *and of the* FREE AND INDEPENDANT STATES OF AMERICA.

THE REPUBLICAN PROCLAMATION[4]

"BRETHREN AND FELLOW CITIZENS:

"The serene tranquillity, the mutual confidence which prevailed amongst us, during the time of the late King's escape, the indifference with which we beheld him return, are unequivocal proofs that the absence of a King is more desirable than his presence, and that he is not only a political superfluity, but a grievous burden, pressing hard on the whole nation.

"Let us not be imposed on by sophisms; all that concerns this is reduced to four points.

"He has abdicated the throne in having fled from his post. Abdication and desertion are not characterized by the length of absence; but by the single act of flight. In the present instance, the act is everything, and the time nothing.

"The nation can never give back its confidence to a man who, false to his trust, perjured to his oath, conspires a clandestine flight, obtains a fraudulent passport, conceals a King of France under the disguise of a valet, directs his course towards a frontier covered with traitors and deserters, and evidently meditates a return into our country, with a force capable of imposing his own despotic laws.

"Should his flight be considered as his own act, or the act of those who fled with him? Was it a spontaneous resolution of his own, or was it inspired by others? The alternative is immaterial; whether fool or hypocrite, idiot or traitor, he has proved himself equally unworthy of the important functions that had been delegated to him.

[4] This manifesto with which Paris was found placarded on July 1, 1791, is described by Dumont as a "Republican Proclamation," but what its literal caption was I have not found. —Conway

"In every sense in which the question can be considered, the reciprocal obligation which subsisted between us is dissolved. He holds no longer any authority. We owe him no longer obedience. We see in him no more than an indifferent person; we can regard him only as Louis Capet.

"The history of France presents little else than a long series of public calamity, which takes its source from the vices of Kings; we have been the wretched victims that have never ceased to suffer either for them or by them. The catalogue of their oppressions was complete, but to complete the sum of their crimes, treason was yet wanting. Now the only vacancy is filled up, the dreadful list is full; the system is exhausted; there are no remaining errors for them to commit; their reign is consequently at an end.

"What kind of office must that be in a government which requires for its execution neither experience nor ability, that may be abandoned to the desperate chance of birth, that may be filled by an idiot, a madman, a tyrant, with equal effect as by the good, the virtuous, and the wise? An office of this nature is a mere nonentity; it is a place of show, not of use. Let France then, arrived at the age of reason, no longer be deluded by the sound of words, and let her deliberately examine, if a King, however insignificant and contemptible in himself, may not at the same time be extremely dangerous.

"The thirty millions which it costs to support a King in the éclat of stupid brutal luxury, presents us with an easy method of reducing taxes, which reduction would at once relieve the people, and stop the progress of political corruption. The grandeur of nations consists, not, as Kings pretend, in the splendour of thrones, but in a conspicuous sense of their own dignity, and in a just disdain of those barbarous follies and crimes which, under the sanction of Royalty, have hitherto desolated Europe.

"As to the personal safety of Louis Capet, it is so much the more confirmed, as France will not stoop to degrade herself by a spirit of revenge against a wretch who has dishonoured himself. In defending a just and glorious cause, it is not possible to degrade it, and the universal tranquillity which prevails is an undeniable proof that a free people know how to respect themselves."

ANTI-MONARCHAL ESSAY

For the Use of New Republicans[5]

When we reach some great good, long desired, we begin by felicitating ourselves. We triumph, we give ourselves up to this joy without rendering to our minds any full account of our reasons for it. Then comes reflection: we pass in review all the circumstances of our new happiness; we compare it in detail with our former condition; and each of these thoughts becomes a fresh enjoyment. This satisfaction, elucidated and well-considered, we now desire to procure for our readers.

In seeing Royalty abolished and the Republic established, all France has resounded with unanimous plaudits.[6] Yet some who clap their hands do not sufficiently understand the condition they are leaving or that which they are assuming.

---

[5] Translated for this work from *Le Patriote François*, Samedi 20 Octobre, 1793, l'an 1er de la République. Supplement au No. 1167, in the Bibliothèque Nationale, Paris. It is headed, "Essai Anti-Monarchique, à L'Usage des Nouveaux Républicains, Tiré de la Feuille Villageoise." I have not found this Feuille, but no doubt Brissot, in editing the essay for his journal (*Le Patriote François*) abridged it, and in one instance Paine is mentioned by name. Although in this essay Paine occasionally repeats sentences used elsewhere, and naturally maintains his well-known principles, the work has a peculiar interest as indicating the temper and visions of the opening revolution. —Conway

[6] Royalty was abolished by the National Convention on the first day of its meeting, September 21, 1792, the revolutionary Calendar beginning next day. Paine was chosen by his fellow-deputies of Calais to congratulate the Convention, and did so in a brief address, dated October 27, which was loaned by M. Charavay to the Historical Exposition of the Revolution at Paris, 1889, where I made the subjoined translation:

The perjuries of Louis, the conspiracies of his court, the wildness of his worthy brothers, have filled every Frenchman with horror, and this race was dethroned in their hearts before its fall by legal decree. But it is little to throw down an idol; it is the pedestal that above all must be broken down; it is the regal office rather than the incumbent that is murderous. All do not realize this.

Why is *Royalty* an absurd and detestable government? Why is the *Republic* a government accordant with nature and reason? At the present time a Frenchman should put himself in a position to answer these two questions clearly. For, in fine, if you are free and contented it is yet needful that you should know why.

Let us first discuss Royalty or Monarchy. Although one often wishes to distinguish between these names, common usage gives them the same sense.

"CITIZEN PRESIDENT: In the name of the Deputies of the Department of the Pas de Calais, I have the honor of presenting to the Convention the felicitations of the General Council of the Commune of Calais on the abolition of Royalty.

"Amid the joy inspired by this event, one cannot forbear some pain at the folly of our ancestors, who have placed us under the necessity of treating gravely (*solennellement*) the abolition of a phantom (*fantôme*).—THOMAS PAINE, Deputy."

—Conway

Royalty

Bands of brigands unite to subvert a country, place it under tribute, seize its lands, enslave its inhabitants. The expedition completed, the chieftain of the robbers adopts the title of monarch or king. Such is the origin of Royalty among all tribes—huntsmen, agriculturists, shepherds.

A second brigand arrives who finds it equitable to take away by force what was conquered by violence: he dispossesses the first; he chains him, kills him, reigns in his place. Ere long time effaces the memory of this origin; the successors rule under a new form; they do a little good, from policy; they corrupt all who surround them; they invent fictitious genealogies to make their families sacred;[7] the knavery of priests comes

[7] The Boston *Investigator*'s compilation of Paine's Works contains the following "as supposed to be Mr. Paine's":

> "Royal Pedigree.—George the Third, who was the grandson of George the Second, who was the son of George the First, who was the son of the Princess Sophia, who was the cousin of Anne, who was the sister of William and Mary, who were the daughter and son-in-law of James the Second, who was the son of Charles the First, who was a traitor to his country and decapitated as such, who was the son of James the First, who was the son of Mary, who was the sister of Edward the Sixth, who was the son of Henry the Eighth, who was the cold-blooded murderer of his wives, and the promoter of the Protestant religion, who was the son of Henry the Seventh, who slew Richard the Third, who smothered his nephew Edward the Fifth, who was the son of Edward the Fourth, who with bloody Richard slew Henry the Sixth, who succeeded Henry the Fifth, who was the son of Henry the Fourth, who was the cousin of Richard the Second, who was the son of Edward the Third, who was the son of Richard the Second, who was the son of Edward the First, who was the son of Henry the Third, who was the son of John, who was the brother of Richard the First, who was the son of Henry the Second, who was the son of Matilda, who

to their aid; they take Religion for a lifeguard: thenceforth tyranny becomes immortal, the usurped power becomes an hereditary right.

The effects of Royalty have been entirely harmonious with its origin. What scenes of horror, what refinements of iniquity, do the annals of monarchies present! If we should paint human nature with a baseness of heart, an hypocrisy, from which all must recoil and humanity disavow, it would be the portraiture of kings, their ministers and courtiers.

And why should it not be so? What should such a monstrosity produce but miseries and crimes? What is monarchy? It has been finely disguised, and the people familiarized with the odious title: in its real sense the word signifies *the absolute power of one single individual*, who may with impunity be stupid, treacherous, tyrannical, etc. Is it not an insult to nations to wish them so governed?

Government by a single individual is vicious in itself, independently of the individual's vices. For however little a State, the prince is nearly always too small: where is the proportion between one man and the affairs of a whole nation?

True, some men of genius have been seen under the diadem; but the evil is then even greater: the ambition of such a man impels him to conquest and despotism, his subjects soon have to lament his glory, and sing their Te-Deums while perishing with hunger. Such is the history of Louis XIV and so many others.

But if ordinary men in power repay you with incapacity or with princely vices? But those who come to the front in monarchies are frequently mere mean mischief-makers, commonplace knaves, petty intriguers, whose small wits, which in courts reach large places, serve only to display their ineptitude in public, as soon as they appear.[8] In short, monarchs do nothing, and their ministers do evil: this is the history of all monarchies.

But if Royalty as such is baneful, as hereditary succession it is equally revolting and ridiculous. What! there exists among my kind a man who pretends that he is born to govern me? Whence derived he

---

was the daughter of Henry the First, who was the brother of William Rufus, who was the son of William the Conqueror, who was the son of a whore."

—Conway

[8] J. J. Rousseau, *Contrat Social.*

such right? From his and my ancestors, says he. But how could they transmit to him a right they did not possess? Man has no authority over generations unborn. I cannot be the slave of the dead, more than of the living. Suppose that instead of our posterity, it was we who should succeed ourselves: we should not today be able to despoil ourselves of the rights which would belong to us in our second life: for a stronger reason we cannot so despoil others.

An hereditary crown! A transmissible throne! What a notion! With even a little reflection, can anyone tolerate it? Should human beings then be the property of certain individuals, born or to be born? Are we then to treat our descendants in advance as cattle, who shall have neither will nor rights of their own? To inherit government is to inherit peoples, as if they were herds. It is the basest, the most shameful fantasy that ever degraded mankind.

It is wrong to reproach kings with their ferocity, their brutal indifference, the oppressions of the people, and molestations of citizens: it is hereditary succession that makes them what they are: this breeds monsters as a marsh breeds vipers.

The logic on which the hereditary prince rests is in effect this: I derive my power from my birth; I derive my birth from God; therefore I owe nothing to men. It is little that he has at hand a complacent minister, he continues to indulge, conscientiously, in all the crimes of tyranny. This has been seen in all times and countries.

Tell me, then, what is there in common between him who is master of a people, and the people of whom he is master? Are these masters really of their kind? It is by sympathy that we are good and human: with whom does a monarch sympathize? When my neighbor suffers I pity, because I put myself in his place: a monarch pities none, because he has never been, can never be, in any other place than his own.

A monarch is an egoist by nature, the egoist *par excellence*. A thousand traits show that this kind of men have no point of contact with the rest of humanity. There was demanded of Charles II the punishment of Lauderdale, his favorite, who had infamously oppressed the Scotch. "Yes," said Charles coolly, "this man has done much against the Scotch, but I cannot see that he has done anything against my interests." Louis XIV often said: "If I follow the wishes of the people, I cannot act the king." Even such phrases as "misfortunes of the State," "safety of the State," filled Louis XIV with wrath.

Could nature make a law which should assure virtue and wisdom invariably in these privileged castes that perpetuate themselves on thrones, there would be no objection to their hereditary succession. But let us pass Europe in review: all of its monarchs are the meanest of men. This one a tyrant, that one an imbecile, another a traitor, the next a debauchee, while some muster all the vices. It looks as if fate and nature had aimed to show our epoch, and all nations, the absurdity and enormity of Royalty.

But I mistake: this epoch has nothing peculiar. For, such is the essential vice of this royal succession by animal filiation, the peoples have not even the chances of nature—they cannot even hope for a good prince as an alternative. All things conspire to deprive of reason and justice an individual reared to command others. The word of young Dionysius was very sensible: his father, reproaching him for a shameful action, said, "Have I given thee such example?" "Ah," answered the youth, "thy father was not a king!"

In truth, were laughter on such a subject permissible, nothing would suggest ideas more burlesque than this fantastic institution of hereditary kings. Would it not be believed, to look at them, that there really exist particular lineages possessing certain qualities which enter the blood of the embryo prince, and adapt him physically for royalty, as a horse for the racecourse? But then, in this wild supposition, it yet becomes necessary to assure the genuine family descent of the heir presumptive. To perpetuate the noble race of Andalusian chargers, the circumstances pass before witnesses, and similar precautions seem necessary, however indecent, to make sure that the trickeries of queens shall not supply thrones with bastards, and that the kings, like the horses, shall always be thoroughbreds.

Whether one jests or reasons, there is found in this idea of hereditary royalty only folly and shame. What then is this office, which may be filled by infants or idiots? Some talent is required to be a simple workman; to be a king there is need to have only the human shape, to be a living automaton. We are astonished when reading that the Egyptians placed on the throne a flint, and called it their king. We smile at the dog Barkouf, sent by an Asiatic despot to govern one of his provinces.[9] But monarchs

[9] See the first year of *La Feuille Villageoise*, No. 42.[Cf. Montaigne's *Essays*, chap. xii. —Conway]

of this kind are less mischievous and less absurd than those before whom whole peoples prostrate themselves. The flint and the dog at least imposed on nobody. None ascribed to them qualities or characters they did not possess. They were not styled "Father of the People,"—though this were hardly more ridiculous than to give that title to a rattle-head whom inheritance crowns at eighteen. Better a mute than an animate idol. Why, there can hardly be cited an instance of a great man having children worthy of him, yet you will have the royal function pass from father to son! As well declare that a wise man's son will be wise. A king is an administrator, and an hereditary administrator is as absurd as an author by birthright.

Royalty is thus as contrary to common sense as to common right. But it would be a plague even if no more than an absurdity; for a people who can bow down in honor of a silly thing is a debased people. Can they be fit for great affairs who render equal homage to vice and virtue, and yield the same submission to ignorance and wisdom? Of all institutions, none has caused more intellectual degeneracy. This explains the often-remarked abjectness of character under monarchies.

Such is also the effect of this contagious institution that it renders equality impossible, and draws in its train the presumption and the evils of "Nobility." If you admit inheritance of an office, why not that of a distinction? The Nobility's heritage asks only homage, that of the Crown commands submission. When a man says to me, "I am born illustrious," I merely smile; when he says "I am born your master," I set my foot on him.

When the Convention pronounced the abolition of Royalty none rose for the defence that was expected. On this subject a philosopher, who thought discussion should always precede enactment, proposed a singular thing; he desired that the Convention should nominate an orator commissioned to plead before it the cause of Royalty, so that the pitiful arguments by which it has in all ages been justified might appear in broad daylight. Judges give one accused, however certain his guilt, an official defender. In the ancient Senate of Venice there existed a public officer whose function was to contest all propositions, however incontestible, or however perfect their evidence. For the rest, pleaders for Royalty are not rare: let us open them, and see what the most specious of royalist reasoners have said.

1. *A king is necessary to preserve a people from the tyranny of powerful men.*
   Establish the Rights of Man;[10] enthrone Equality; form a good Constitution; divide well its powers; let there be no privileges, no distinctions of birth, no monopolies; make safe the liberty of industry and of trade, the equal distribution of [family] inheritances, publicity of administration, freedom of the press: these things all established, you will be assured of good laws, and need not fear the powerful men. Willingly or unwillingly, all citizens will be under the Law.
2. *The Legislature might usurp authority, and a king is needed to restrain it.*
   With representatives, frequently renewed, who neither administer nor judge, whose functions are determined by the laws; with national conventions, with primary assemblies, which can be convoked any moment; with a people knowing how to read, and how to defend itself; with good journals, guns, and pikes; a Legislature would have a good deal of trouble in enjoying any months of tyranny. Let us not suppose an evil for the sake of its remedy.
3. *A king is needed to give force to executive power.*
   This might be said while there existed nobles, a priesthood, parliaments, the privileged of every kind. But at present who can resist the Law, which is the will of all, whose execution is the interest of all? On the contrary the existence of an hereditary prince inspires perpetual distrust among the friends of liberty; his authority is odious to them; in checking despotism they constantly obstruct the action of government. Observe how feeble the executive power was found, after our recent pretence of marrying Royalty with Liberty.

Take note, for the rest, that those who talk in this way are men who believe that the King and the Executive Power are only one and the same thing: readers of *La Feuille Villageoise* are more advanced.[11]

---

[10] The reader should bear in mind that this phrase, now used vaguely, had for Paine and his political school a special significance; it implied a fundamental Declaration of individual rights, of supreme force and authority, invasion which, either by legislatures, law courts, majorities, or administrators, was to be regarded as the worst treason and despotism. —Conway

[11] See No. 50.

Others use this bad reasoning: "Were there no hereditary chief there would be an elective chief: the citizens would side with this man or that, and there would be a civil war at every election." In the first place, it is certain that hereditary succession alone has produced the civil wars of France and England; and that beyond this are the pretended rights, of royal families which have twenty times drawn on these nations the scourge of foreign wars. It is, in fine, the heredity of crowns that has caused the troubles of Regency, which Thomas Paine calls Monarchy at nurse.

But above all it must be said, that if there be an elective chief, that chief will not be a king surrounded by courtiers, burdened with pomp, inflated by idolatries, and endowed with thirty millions of money; also, that no citizen will be tempted to injure himself by placing another citizen, his equal, for some years in an office without limited income and circumscribed power.

In a word, whoever demands a king demands an aristocracy, and thirty millions of taxes. See why Franklin described Royalism as *a crime like poisoning*.

Royalty, its fanatical éclat, its superstitious idolatry, the delusive assumption of its necessity, all these fictions have been invented only to obtain from men excessive taxes and voluntary servitude. Royalty and Popery have had the same aim, have sustained themselves by the same artifices, and crumble under the same Light.

DECLARATION OF RIGHTS[12]

The object of all union of men in society being maintenance of their natural rights, civil and political, these rights are the basis of the social pact: their recognition and their declaration ought to precede the Constitution which assures their guarantee.

1. The natural rights of men, civil and political, are liberty, equality, security, property, social protection, and resistance to oppression.
2. Liberty consists in the right to do whatever is not contrary to the rights of others: thus, exercise of the natural rights of each individual

[12] In his appeal from prison to the Convention (August 7, 1794) Paine states that he had, as a member of the Committee for framing the Constitution, prepared a Plan, which was in the hands of Barère, also of that Committee. I have not yet succeeded in finding Paine's Constitution, but it is certain that the work of framing the Constitution of 1793 was mainly entrusted to Paine and Condorcet. Dr. John Moore, in his work on the French Revolution, describes the two at their work; and it is asserted that he "assisted in drawing up the French Declaration of Rights," by "Juvencus," author of an able "Essay on the Life and Genius of Thomas Paine," whose information came from a personal friend of Paine. (*Aphorisms, Opinions, and Reflections of Thomas Paine*, etc., London, 1826. Pp. 3, 14.) A translation of the Declaration and Constitution appeared in England (Debrett, Picadilly, 1793), but with some faults. The present translation is from *Œuvres Complètes de Condorcet*, tome xviii. The Committee reported their Constitution February 15th, and April 15th was set for its discussion, Robespierre then demanded separate discussion of the Declaration of Rights, to which he objected that it made no mention of the Supreme Being, and that its extreme principles of freedom would shield illicit traffic. Paine and Jefferson were troubled that the United States Constitution contained no Declaration of Rights, it being a fundamental principle in Paine's theory of government that such a Declaration was the main safeguard of the individual against the despotism of numbers. —Conway

has no limits other than those which secure to other members of society enjoyment of the same rights.

3. The preservation of liberty depends on submission to the Law, which is the expression of the general will. Nothing unforbidden by law can be hindered, and none may be forced to do what the law does not command.
4. Every man is free to make known his thoughts and opinions.
5. Freedom of the press, and every other means of publishing one's opinion, cannot be interdicted, suspended, or limited.
6. Every citizen shall be free in the exercise of his religion (*culte*).
7. Equality consists in the enjoyment by every one of the same rights.
8. The law should be equal for all, whether it rewards or punishes, protects or represses.
9. All citizens are admissible to all public positions, employments, and functions. Free nations recognize no grounds of preference save talents and virtues.
10. Security consists in the protection accorded by society to every citizen for the preservation of his person, property, and rights.
11. None should be sued, accused, arrested, or detained, save in cases determined by the law, and in accordance with forms prescribed by it. Every other act against a citizen is arbitrary and null.
12. Those who solicit, further, sign, execute, or cause to be executed, such arbitrary acts are culpable, and should be punished.
13. Citizens against whom the execution of such acts is attempted have the right to repel force by force; but every citizen summoned or arrested by authority of the Law, and in the forms by it prescribed, should instantly obey: he renders himself guilty by resistance.
14. Every man being presumed innocent until legally pronounced guilty, should his arrest be deemed indispensable, all rigor not necessary to secure his person should be severely repressed by law.
15. None should be punished save in virtue of a law formally enacted, promulgated anterior to the offence, and legally applied.
16. Any law that should punish offences committed before its existence would be an arbitrary act. Retroactive effect given to the law is a crime.
17. The law should award only penalties strictly and evidently necessary to the general safety. Penalties should be proportioned to offences, and useful to society.

18. The right of property consists in every man's being master in the disposal, at his will, of his goods, capital, income, and industry.
19. No kind of labor, commerce, or culture, can be prohibited to anyone: he may make, sell, and transport every species of production.
20. Every man may engage his services and his time; but he cannot sell himself; his person is not an alienable property.
21. No one can be deprived of the least portion of his property without his consent, unless evidently required by public necessity, legally determined, and under the condition of a just indemnity in advance.
22. No tax shall be imposed except for the general welfare, and to meet public needs. All citizens have the right to unite personally, or by their representatives, in the fixing of imposts.
23. Instruction is the need of all, and society owes it to all its members equally.
24. Public succours are a sacred debt of society; it is for the law to determine their extent and application.
25. The social guarantee of the rights of man rests on the national sovereignty.
26. This sovereignty is one, indivisible, imprescriptible, and inalienable.
27. It resides essentially in the whole people, and every citizen has an equal right to unite in its exercise.
28. No partial assemblage of citizens, and no individual, may attribute to themselves sovereignty, or exercise any authority, or discharge any public function, without formal delegation thereto by the law.
29. The social guarantee cannot exist if the limits of public administration are not clearly determined by law, and if the responsibility of all public functionaries is not assured.
30. All citizens are bound to unite in this guarantee, and in enforcing the law when summoned in its name.
31. Men united in society should have legal means of resisting oppression.
32. There is oppression when any law violates the natural rights, civil and political, which it should guarantee.

    There is oppression when the law is violated by public officials in its application to individual cases.

    There is oppression when arbitrary actions violate the rights of citizen against the express purpose (*expression*) of the law.

In a free government the mode of resisting these different acts of oppression should be regulated by the Constitution.

33. A people possesses always the right to reform and alter its Constitution. A generation has no right to subject a future generation to its laws; and all heredity in offices is absurd and tyrannical.

DISSERTATION ON FIRST PRINCIPLES OF GOVERNMENT[13]

There is no subject more interesting to every man than the subject of government. His security, be he rich or poor, and in a great measure his prosperity, are connected therewith; it is therefore his interest as well as his duty to make himself acquainted with its principles, and what the practice ought to be.

Every art and science, however imperfectly known at first, has been studied, improved, and brought to what we call perfection by the progressive labours of succeeding generations; but the science of government has stood still. No improvement has been made in the principle and scarcely any in the practice till the American revolution began. In all the countries of Europe (except in France) the same forms

---

[13] Printed from the first edition, whose title is as above, with the addition: "By Thomas Paine, Author of Common Sense; Rights of Man; Age of Reason. Paris, Printed at the English Press, rue de Vaugerard, No. 970. Third year of the French Republic." The pamphlet seems to have appeared early in July (perhaps the Fourth), 1795, and was meant to influence the decision of the National Convention on the Constitution then under discussion. This Constitution, adopted September 23rd, presently swept away by Napoleon, contained some features which appeared to Paine reactionary. Those to which he most objected are quoted by him in his speech in the Convention, which is bound up in the same pamphlet, and follows this "Dissertation" in the present volume. In the Constitution as adopted Paine's preference for a plural Executive was established, and though the bicameral organization (the Council of Five Hundred and the Council of Ancients) was not such as he desired, his chief objection was based on his principle of manhood suffrage. But in regard to this see Paine's "Dissertations on Government," written nine years before, where he indicates the method of restraining the despotism of numbers. —Conway

and systems that were erected in the remote ages of ignorance still continue, and their antiquity is put in the place of principle; it is forbidden to investigate their origin, or by what right they exist. If it be asked how has this happened, the answer is easy: they are established on a principle that is false, and they employ their power to prevent detection.

Notwithstanding the mystery with which the science of government has been enveloped, for the purpose of enslaving, plundering, and imposing upon mankind, it is of all things the least mysterious and the most easy to be understood. The meanest capacity cannot be at a loss, if it begins its enquiries at the right point. Every art and science has some point, or alphabet, at which the study of that art or science begins, and by the assistance of which the progress is facilitated. The same method ought to be observed with respect to the science of government.

Instead then of embarrassing the subject in the outset with the numerous subdivisions under which different forms of government have been classed, such as aristocracy, democracy, oligarchy, monarchy, etc. the better method will be to begin with what may be called primary divisions, or those under which all the several subdivisions will be comprehended.

The primary divisions are but two:

First, government by election and representation.

Secondly, government by hereditary succession.

All the several forms and systems of government, however numerous or diversified, class themselves under one or other of those primary divisions; for either they are on the system of representation, or on that of hereditary succession. As to that equivocal thing called mixed government, such as the late government of Holland, and the present government of England, it does not make an exception to the general rule, because the parts separately considered are either representative or hereditary.

Beginning then our enquiries at this point, we have first to examine into the nature of those two primary divisions.

If they are equally right in principle, it is mere matter of opinion which we prefer. If the one be demonstratively better than the other, that difference directs our choice; but if one of them should be so absolutely false as not to have a right to existence, the matter settles itself at once; because a negative proved on one thing, where two only are offered, and one must be accepted, amounts to an affirmative on the other.

The revolutions that are now spreading themselves in the world have their origin in this state of the case, and the present war is a conflict between the representative system founded on the rights of the people, and the hereditary system founded in usurpation. As to what are called Monarchy, Royalty, and Aristocracy, they do not, either as things or as terms, sufficiently describe the hereditary system; they are but secondary things or signs of the hereditary system, and which fall of themselves if that system has not a right to exist. Were there no such terms as Monarchy, Royalty, and Aristocracy, or were other terms substituted in their place, the hereditary system, if it continued, would not be altered thereby. It would be the same system under any other titulary name as it is now.

The character therefore of the revolutions of the present day distinguishes itself most definitively by grounding itself on the system of representative government, in opposition to the hereditary. No other distinction reaches the whole of the principle.

Having thus opened the case generally, I proceed, in the first place, to examine the hereditary system, because it has the priority in point of time. The representative system is the invention of the modern world; and, that no doubt may arise as to my own opinion, I declare it before hand, which is, *that there is not a problem in Euclid more mathematically true, than that hereditary government has not a right to exist. When therefore we take from any man the exercise of hereditary power, we take away that which he never had the right to possess, and which no law or custom could, or ever can, give him a title to.*

The arguments that have hitherto been employed against the hereditary system have been chiefly founded upon the absurdity of it, and its incompetency to the purpose of good government. Nothing can present to our judgment, or to our imagination, a figure of greater absurdity, than that of seeing the government of a nation fall, as it frequently does, into the hands of a lad necessarily destitute of experience, and often little better than a fool. It is an insult to every man of years, of character, and of talents, in a country. The moment we begin to reason upon the hereditary system, it falls into derision; let but a single idea begin, and a thousand will soon follow. Insignificance, imbecility, childhood, dotage, want of moral character; in fine, every defect serious or laughable unite to hold up the hereditary system as a figure of ridicule. Leaving, however, the ridiculousness of the thing to the reflections of the reader, I proceed to the more important part of the question, namely, whether such a system has a right to exist.

To be satisfied of the right of a thing to exist, we must be satisfied that it had a right to begin. If it had not a right to begin, it has not a right to continue. By what right then did the hereditary system begin? Let a man but ask himself this question, and he will find that he cannot satisfy himself with an answer.

The right which any man or any family had to set itself up at first to govern a nation, and to establish itself hereditarily, was no other than the right which Robespierre had to do the same thing in France. If he had none, they had none. If they had any, he had as much; for it is impossible to discover superiority of right in any family, by virtue of which hereditary government could begin. The Capets, the Guelphs, the Robespierres, the Marats, are all on the same standing as to the question of right. It belongs exclusively to none.

It is one step towards liberty, to perceive that hereditary government could not begin as an exclusive right in any family. The next point will be, whether, having once begun, it could grow into a right by the influence of time.

This would be supposing an absurdity; for either it is putting time in the place of principle, or making it superior to principle; whereas time has no more connection with, or influence upon principle, than principle has upon time. The wrong which began a thousand years ago, is as much a wrong as if it began today; and the right which originates today, is as much a right as if it had the sanction of a thousand years. Time with respect to principles is an eternal now: it has no operation upon them: it changes nothing of their nature and qualities. But what have we to do with a thousand years? Our lifetime is but a short portion of that period, and if we find the wrong in existence as soon as we begin to live, that is the point of time at which it begins to us; and our right to resist it is the same as if it never existed before.

As hereditary government could not begin as a natural right in any family, nor derive after its commencement any right from time, we have only to examine whether there exist in a nation a right to set it up, and establish it by what is called law, as has been done in England. I answer NO; and that any law or any constitution made for that purpose is an act of treason against the right of every minor in the nation, at the time it is made, and against the rights of all succeeding generations. I shall speak upon each of those cases. First, of the minor at the time such law is made. Secondly, of the generations that are to follow.

A nation, in a collective sense, comprehends all the individuals of whatever age, from just born to just dying. Of these, one part will be minors, and the other aged. The average of life is not exactly the same in every climate and country, but in general, the minority in years are the majority in numbers; that is, the number of persons under twenty-one years, is greater than the number of persons above that age. This difference in number is not necessary to the establishment of the principle I mean to lay down, but it serves to show the justice of it more strongly. The principle would be equally as good, if the majority in years were also the majority in numbers.

The rights of minors are as sacred as the rights of the aged. The difference is altogether in the different age of the two parties, and nothing in the nature of the rights; the rights are the same rights; and are to be preserved inviolate for the inheritance of the minors when they shall come of age. During the minority of minors their rights are under the sacred guardianship of the aged. The minor cannot surrender them; the guardian cannot dispossess him; consequently, the aged part of a nation, who are the lawmakers for the time being, and who, in the march of life are but a few years ahead of those who are yet minors, and to whom they must shortly give place, have not and cannot have the right to make a law to set up and establish hereditary government, or, to speak more distinctly, *an hereditary succession of governors*; because it is an attempt to deprive every minor in the nation, at the time such a law is made, of his inheritance of rights when he shall come of age, and to subjugate him to a system of government to which, during his minority, he could neither consent nor object.

If a person who is a minor at the time such a law is proposed, had happened to have been born a few years sooner, so as to be of the age of twenty-one years at the time of proposing it, his right to have objected against it, to have exposed the injustice and tyrannical principles of it, and to have voted against it, will be admitted on all sides. If, therefore, the law operates to prevent his exercising the same rights after he comes of age as he would have had a right to exercise had he been of age at the time, it is undeniably a law to take away and annul the rights of every person in the nation who shall be a minor at the time of making such a law, and consequently the right to make it cannot exist.

I come now to speak of government by hereditary succession, as it applies to succeeding generations; and to show that in this case, as in the case of minors, there does not exist in a nation a right to set it up.

A nation, though continually existing, is continually in a state of renewal and succession. It is never stationary.

Every day produces new births, carries minors forward to maturity, and old persons from the stage. In this ever running flood of generations there is no part superior in authority to another. Could we conceive an idea of superiority in any, at what point of time, or in what century of the world, are we to fix it? To what cause are we to ascribe it? By what evidence are we to prove it? By what criterion are we to know it? A single reflection will teach us that our ancestors, like ourselves, were but tenants for life in the great freehold of rights. The fee-absolute was not in them, it is not in us, it belongs to the whole family of man, thro' all ages. If we think otherwise than this, we think either as slaves or as tyrants. As slaves, if we think that any former generation had a right to bind us; as tyrants, if we think that we have authority to bind the generations that are to follow.

It may not be inapplicable to the subject, to endeavour to define what is to be understood by a generation, in the sense the word is here used.

As a natural term its meaning is sufficiently clear. The father, the son, the grandson, are so many distinct generations. But when we speak of a generation as describing the persons in whom legal authority resides, as distinct from another generation of the same description who are to succeed them, it comprehends all those who are above the age of twenty-one years, at the time that we count from; and a generation of this kind will continue in authority between fourteen and twenty-one years, that is, until the number of minors, who shall have arrived at age, shall be greater than the number of persons remaining of the former stock.

For example: if France, at this or any other moment, contains twenty-four millions of souls, twelve millions will be males, and twelve females. Of the twelve millions of males, six millions will be of the age of twenty-one years, and six will be under, and the authority to govern will reside in the first six. But every day will make some alteration, and in twenty-one years every one of those minors who survives will have arrived at age, and the greater part of the former stock will be gone: the majority of persons then living, in whom the legal authority resides, will be composed of those who, twenty-one years before, had no legal existence. Those will be fathers and grandfathers in their turn, and, in the next twenty-one years, (or less) another race of minors, arrived at age, will succeed them, and so on.

As this is ever the case, and as every generation is equal in rights to another, it consequently follows, that there cannot be a right in any to establish government by hereditary succession, because it would be supposing itself possessed of a right superior to the rest, namely, that of commanding by its own authority how the world shall be hereafter governed and who shall govern it. Every age and generation is, and must be, (as a matter of right,) as free to act for itself in all cases, as the age and generation that preceded it. The vanity and presumption of governing beyond the grave is the most ridiculous and insolent of all tyrannies. Man has no property in man, neither has one generation a property in the generations that are to follow.

In the first part of the *Rights of Man* I have spoken of government by hereditary succession; and I will here close the subject with an extract from that work, which states it under the two following heads.

> First, The right of a particular Family to establish itself.
>
> Secondly, The right of a Nation to establish a particular Family.
>
> With respect to the *first* of these heads, that of a Family establishing itself with hereditary powers on its own authority, and independent of the consent of a Nation, all men will concur in calling it despotism; and it would be trespassing on their understanding to attempt to prove it.
>
> But the *second* head, that of a Nation establishing a particular Family with *hereditary powers*, does not present itself as despotism on the first reflection; but if men will permit it a second reflection to take place, and carry that reflection forward but one remove out of their own persons to that of their offspring, they will then see that hereditary succession becomes in its consequences the same despotism to others, which they reprobated for themselves. It operates to preclude the consent of the succeeding generations; and the preclusion of consent is despotism. When the person who at any time

shall be in possession of a Government, or those who stand in succession to him, shall say to a Nation, I hold this power in "contempt" of you, it signifies not on what authority he pretends to say it. It is no relief, but an aggravation to a person in slavery, to reflect that he was sold by his parent; and as that which heightens the criminality of an act cannot be produced to prove the legality of it, hereditary succession cannot be established as a legal thing.

In order to arrive at a more perfect decision on this head, it will be proper to consider the generation which undertakes to establish a Family with *hereditary powers*, apart and separate from the generations which are to follow; and also to consider the character in which the *first* generation acts with respect to succeeding generations.

The generation which first selects a person, and puts him at the head of its Government, either with the title of King, or any other distinction, acts on its own choice, be it wise or foolish, as a free agent for itself. The person so set up is not hereditary, but selected and appointed; and the generation who sets him up, does not live under a hereditary government, but under a government of its own choice and establishment. Were the generation who sets him up, and the person so set up, to live forever, it never could become hereditary succession; and of consequence hereditary succession can only follow on the death of the first parties.

As, therefore, hereditary succession is out of the question with respect to the *first* generation, we have now to consider the character in which that generation acts with respect to the commencing generation, and to all succeeding ones.

It assumes a character, to which it has neither right nor title. It changes itself from a *Legislator* to a *Testator*, and effects to make its Will, which is to have operation after the demise of the makers, to bequeath the Government; and it not only attempts to bequeath, but to establish on the succeeding generation, a new and different form of Government under which itself lived. Itself, as already observed, lived not under a hereditary Government but under a Government of its own choice and establishment; and it now attempts, by virtue of a will and testament (and which it has not authority to make), to take from the commencing generation, and all future ones, the rights and free agency by which itself acted.

But, exclusive of the right which any generation has to act collectively as a testator, the objects to which it applies itself in this case, are not within the compass of any law, or of any will or testament.

The rights of men in society, are neither devisable or transferable, nor annihilable, but are descendable only, and it is not in the power of any generation to intercept finally, and cut off the descent. If the present generation, or any other, are disposed to be slaves, it does not lessen the right of the succeeding generation to be free. Wrongs cannot have a legal descent. When Mr. Burke attempts to maintain that the "English nation did at the Revolution of 1688, most solemnly renounce and abdicate their rights for themselves, and for all their posterity forever," he speaks a language that merits not reply, and which can only excite contempt for his prostitute principles, or pity for his ignorance.

In whatever light hereditary succession, as growing out of the will and testament of some former generation, presents itself, it is an absurdity. A cannot make a will to take from B the property of B, and give it to C; yet this is the manner in which (what is called) hereditary succession by law operates. A certain former generation made a will, to take away the rights of the commencing generation, and all future ones, and convey those rights to a third person, who afterwards comes forward, and tells them, in Mr. Burke's language, that they have *no rights*, that their rights are already bequeathed to him and that he will govern in *contempt* of them. From such principles, and such ignorance, good Lord deliver the world!

The history of the English parliament furnishes an example of this kind; and which merits to be recorded, as being the greatest instance of legislative ignorance and want of principle that is to be found in any country. The case is as follows:

The English parliament of 1688, imported a man and his wife from Holland, *William* and *Mary*, and made them king and queen of

England.[14] Having done this, the said parliament made a law to convey the government of the country to the heirs of William and Mary, in the following words: "We, the lords spiritual and temporal, and commons, do, in the name of the people of England, most humbly and faithfully submit *ourselves, our heirs, and posterities*, to William and Mary, *their heirs and posterities*, forever." And in a subsequent law, as quoted by Edmund Burke, the said parliament, in the name of the people of England then living, *binds the said people, their heirs and posterities, to William and Mary, their heirs and posterities, to the end of time.*

It is not sufficient that we laugh at the ignorance of such lawmakers; it is necessary that we reprobate their want of principle. The constituent assembly of France, 1789, fell into the same vice as the parliament of England had done, and assumed to establish an hereditary succession in the family of the Capets, as an act of the constitution of that year. That every nation, *for the time being*, has a right to govern itself as it pleases, must always be admitted; but government by hereditary succession is government for another race of people, and not for itself; and as those on whom it is to operate are not yet in existence, or are minors, so neither is the right in existence to set it up for them, and to assume such a right is treason against the right of posterity.

I here close the arguments on the first head, that of government by hereditary succession; and proceed to the second, that of government by election and representation; or, as it may be concisely expressed, *representative government*, in contradistinction to *hereditary government*.

Reasoning by exclusion, if *hereditary government* has not a right to exist, and that it has not is proveable, *representative government* is admitted of course.

In contemplating government by election and representation, we amuse not ourselves in enquiring when or how, or by what right, it began. Its origin is ever in view. Man is himself the origin and the evidence of

---

[14] "The Bill of Rights (temp. William III) shows that the Lords and Commons met not in Parliament but in convention, that they declared against James II, and in favour of William III. The latter was accepted as sovereign, and, when monarch. Acts of Parliament were passed confirming what had been done."

—*Joseph Fisher in* Notes and Queries *(London), May 2, 1874*

This does not affect Paine's argument, as a Convention could have no more right to bind the future than a Parliament. —Conway

the right. It appertains to him in right of his existence, and his person is the title deed.[15]

The true and only true basis of representative government is equality of Rights. Every man has a right to one vote, and no more, in the choice of representatives. The rich have no more right to exclude the poor from the right of voting, or of electing and being elected, than the poor have to exclude the rich; and wherever it is attempted, or proposed, on either side, it is a question of force and not of right. Who is he that would exclude another? That other has a right to exclude him.

That which is now called aristocracy implies an inequality of rights; but who are the persons that have a right to establish this inequality? Will the rich exclude themselves? No. Will the poor exclude themselves? No. By what right then can any be excluded? It would be a question, if any man or class of men have a right to exclude themselves; but, be this as it may, they cannot have the right to exclude another. The poor will not delegate such a right to the rich, nor the rich to the poor, and to assume it is not only to assume arbitrary power, but to assume a right to commit robbery. Personal rights, of which the right of voting for representatives is one, are a species of property of the most sacred kind: and he that would employ his pecuniary property, or presume upon the influence it gives him, to dispossess or rob another of his property of rights, uses that pecuniary property as he would use firearms, and merits to have it taken from him.

Inequality of rights is created by a combination in one part of the community to exclude another part from its rights. Whenever it be made an article of a constitution, or a law, that the right of voting, or of electing and being elected, shall appertain exclusively to persons possessing a certain quantity of property, be it little or much, it is a combination of

---

[15] "The sacred rights of mankind are not to be rummaged for among old parchments or musty records. They are written as with a sunbeam in the whole volume of human nature by the hand of Divinity itself, and can never be erased or obscured by mortal power."

—*Alexander Hamilton, 1775*

(Cf. *Rights of Man*, vol. ii, p. 304):

> "Portions of antiquity by proving everything establish nothing. It is authority against authority all the way, till we come to the divine origin of the rights of man at the creation."
>
> —Conway

the persons possessing that quantity to exclude those who do not possess the same quantity. It is investing themselves with powers as a self-created part of society, to the exclusion of the rest.

It is always to be taken for granted, that those who oppose an equality of rights never mean the exclusion should take place on themselves; and in this view of the case, pardoning the vanity of the thing, aristocracy is a subject of laughter. This self-soothing vanity is encouraged by another idea not less selfish, which is, that the opposers conceive they are playing a safe game, in which there is a chance to gain and none to lose; that at any rate the doctrine of equality includes *them*, and that if they cannot get more rights than those whom they oppose and would exclude, they shall not have less. This opinion has already been fatal to thousands, who, not contented with *equal rights*, have sought more till they lost all, and experienced in themselves the degrading *inequality* they endeavoured to fix upon others.

In any view of the case it is dangerous and impolitic, sometimes ridiculous, and always unjust, to make property the criterion of the right of voting. If the sum or value of the property upon which the right is to take place be considerable, it will exclude a majority of the people, and unite them in a common interest against the government and against those who support it; and as the power is always with the majority, they can overturn such a government and its supporters whenever they please.

If, in order to avoid this danger, a small quantity of property be fixed, as the criterion of the right, it exhibits liberty in disgrace, by putting it in competition with accident and insignificance. When a broodmare shall fortunately produce a foal or a mule that, by being worth the sum in question, shall convey to its owner the right of voting, or by its death take it from him, in whom does the origin of such a right exist? Is it in the man, or in the mule? When we consider how many ways property may be acquired without merit, and lost without a crime, we ought to spurn the idea of making it a criterion of rights.

But the offensive part of the case is, that this exclusion from the right of voting implies a stigma on the moral character of the persons excluded; and this is what no part of the community has a right to pronounce upon another part. No external circumstance can justify it: wealth is no proof of moral character; nor poverty of the want of it. On the contrary, wealth is often the presumptive evidence of dishonesty; and poverty the negative evidence of innocence. If therefore property, whether little or much, be made a criterion, the means by which that property has been acquired ought to be made a criterion also.

The only ground upon which exclusion from the right of voting is consistent with justice, would be to inflict it as a punishment for a certain time upon those who should propose to take away that right from others. The right of voting for representatives is the primary right by which other rights are protected. To take away this right is to reduce a man to slavery, for slavery consists in being subject to the will of another, and he that has not a vote in the election of representatives is in this case. The proposal therefore to disfranchise any class of men is as criminal as the proposal to take away property. When we speak of right, we ought always to unite with it the idea of duties: rights become duties by reciprocity. The right which I enjoy becomes my duty to guarantee it to another, and he to me; and those who violate the duty justly incur a forfeiture of the right.

In a political view of the case, the strength and permanent security of government is in proportion to the number of people interested in supporting it. The true policy therefore is to interest the whole by an equality of rights, for the danger arises from exclusions. It is possible to exclude men from the right of voting, but it is impossible to exclude them from the right of rebelling against that exclusion; and when all other rights are taken away, the right of rebellion is made perfect.

While men could be persuaded they had no rights, or that rights appertained only to a certain class of men, or that government was a thing existing in right of itself, it was not difficult to govern them authoritatively. The ignorance in which they were held, and the superstition in which they were instructed, furnished the means of doing it. But when the ignorance is gone, and the superstition with it; when they perceive the imposition that has been acted upon them; when they reflect that the cultivator and the manufacturer are the primary means of all the wealth that exists in the world, beyond what nature spontaneously produces; when they begin to feel their consequence by their usefulness, and their right as members of society, it is then no longer possible to govern them as before. The fraud once detected cannot be reacted. To attempt it is to provoke derision, or invite destruction.

That property will ever be unequal is certain. Industry, superiority of talents, dexterity of management, extreme frugality, fortunate opportunities, or the opposite, or the means of those things, will ever produce that effect, without having recourse to the harsh, ill sounding names of avarice and oppression; and besides this, there are some men who, though they do not despise wealth, will not stoop to the drudgery or the means of acquiring it, nor will be troubled with it beyond their wants or their independence; whilst in others there is an avidity to obtain it by every means not punishable; it makes the sole business of their lives, and they follow it as a religion. All that is required with respect to property is to obtain it honestly, and not employ it criminally; but it is always criminally employed when it is made a criterion for exclusive rights.

In institutions that are purely pecuniary, such as that of a bank or a commercial company, the rights of the members composing that company are wholly created by the property they invest therein; and no other rights are represented in the government of that company, than what arise out of that property; neither has that government cognizance of *anything but property*.

But the case is totally different with respect to the institution of civil government, organized on the system of representation. Such a government has cognizance of everything, and of *every man* as a member of the national society, whether he has property or not; and, therefore, the principle requires that *every man*, and *every kind of right*, be represented, of which the right to acquire and to hold property is but one, and that not of the most essential kind. The protection of a man's person is more sacred than the protection of property; and besides this, the faculty of performing any kind of work or services by which he acquires a livelihood, or maintaining his family, is of the nature of property. It is property to him; he has acquired it; and it is as much the object of his protection as exterior property, possessed without that faculty, can be the object of protection in another person.

I have always believed that the best security for property, be it much or little, is to remove from every part of the community, as far as can possibly be done, every cause of complaint, and every motive to violence; and this can only be done by an equality of rights. When rights are secure, property is secure in consequence. But when property is made a pretence for unequal or exclusive rights, it weakens the right to hold the property, and provokes indignation and tumult; for it is unnatural to believe that property can be secure under the guarantee of a society injured in its rights by the influence of that property.

Next to the injustice and ill-policy of making property a pretence for exclusive rights, is the unaccountable absurdity of giving to mere *sound* the idea of property, and annexing to it certain rights; for what else is a *title* but sound? Nature is often giving to the world some extraordinary men who arrive at fame by merit and universal consent, such as Aristotle, Socrates, Plato, etc. They were truly great or noble.

But when government sets up a manufactory of nobles, it is as absurd as if she undertook to manufacture wise men. Her nobles are all counterfeits.

This waxwork order has assumed the name of aristocracy; and the disgrace of it would be lessened if it could be considered only as childish imbecility. We pardon foppery because of its insignificance; and on the same ground we might pardon the foppery of Titles. But the origin of aristocracy was worse than foppery. It was robbery. The first aristocrats in all countries were brigands. Those of later times, sycophants.

It is very well known that in England, (and the same will be found in other countries) the great landed estates now held in descent were plundered from the quiet inhabitants at the conquest. The possibility did not exist of acquiring such estates honestly. If it be asked how they could have been acquired, no answer but that of robbery can be given. That they were not acquired by trade, by commerce, by manufactures, by agriculture, or by any reputable employment, is certain. How then were they acquired? Blush, aristocracy, to hear your origin, for your progenitors were Thieves. They were the Robespierres and the Jacobins of that day. When they had committed the robbery, they endeavoured to lose the disgrace of it by sinking their real names under fictitious ones, which they called Titles. It is ever the practice of Felons to act in this manner. They never pass by their real names.[16]

As property, honestly obtained, is best secured by an equality of Rights, so ill-gotten property depends for protection on a monopoly of rights. He who has robbed another of his property, will next endeavour to disarm him of his rights, to secure that property; for when the robber becomes the legislator he believes himself secure. That part of the government of England that is called the house of lords, was originally composed of persons who had committed the robberies of which I have been speaking. It was an association for the protection of the property they had stolen.

[16] This and the preceding paragraph have been omitted from some editions. —Conway

But besides the criminality of the origin of aristocracy, it has an injurious effect on the moral and physical character of man. Like slavery it debilitates the human faculties; for as the mind bowed down by slavery loses in silence its elastic powers, so, in the contrary extreme, when it is buoyed up by folly, it becomes incapable of exerting them, and dwindles into imbecility. It is impossible that a mind employed upon ribbons and titles can ever be great. The childishness of the objects consumes the man.

It is at all times necessary, and more particularly so during the progress of a revolution, and until right ideas confirm themselves by habit, that we frequently refresh our patriotism by reference to first principles. It is by tracing things to their origin that we learn to understand them: and it is by keeping that line and that origin always in view that we never forget them.

An enquiry into the origin of Rights will demonstrate to us that *rights* are not *gifts* from one man to another, nor from one class of men to another; for who is he who could be the first giver, or by what principle, or on what authority, could he possess the right of giving? A declaration of rights is not a creation of them, nor a donation of them. It is a manifest of the principle by which they exist, followed by a detail of what the rights are; for every civil right has a natural right for its foundation, and it includes the principle of a reciprocal guarantee of those rights from man to man. As, therefore, it is impossible to discover any origin of rights otherwise than in the origin of man, it consequently follows, that rights appertain to man in right of his existence only, and must therefore be equal to every man. The principle of an *equality of rights* is clear and simple. Every man can understand it, and it is by understanding his rights that he learns his duties; for where the rights of men are equal, every man must finally see the necessity of protecting the rights of others as the most effectual security for his own. But if, in the formation of a constitution, we depart from the principle of equal rights, or attempt any modification of it, we plunge into a labyrinth of difficulties from which there is no way out but by retreating. Where are we to stop? Or by what principle are we to find out the point to stop at, that shall discriminate between men of the same country, part of whom shall be free, and the rest not? If property is to be made the criterion, it is a total departure from every moral principle of liberty, because it is attaching rights to mere matter, and making man the agent of that matter. It is, moreover, holding up property as an apple of discord, and not only exciting but justifying war against it; for I maintain the principle, that when property is used as an instrument to take away the rights of those who may happen not to possess property, it is used to an unlawful purpose, as firearms would be in a similar case.

In a state of nature all men are equal in rights, but they are not equal in power; the weak cannot protect themselves against the strong. This being the case, the institution of civil society is for the purpose of making an equalization of powers that shall be parallel to, and a guarantee of, the equality of rights. The laws of a country, when properly constructed, apply to this purpose. Every man takes the arm of the law for his protection as more effectual than his own; and therefore every man has an equal right in the formation of the government, and of the laws by which he is to be governed and judged. In extensive countries and societies, such as America and France, this right in the individual can only be exercised by delegation, that is, by election and representation; and hence it is that the institution of representative government arises.

Hitherto, I have confined myself to matters of principle only. First, that hereditary government has not a right to exist; that it cannot be established on any principle of right; and that it is a violation of all principle. Secondly, that government by election and representation has its origin in the natural and eternal rights of man; for whether a man be his own lawgiver, as he would be in a state of nature; or whether he exercises his portion of legislative sovereignty in his own person, as might be the case in small democracies where all could assemble for the formation of the laws by which they were to be governed; or whether he exercises it in the choice of persons to represent him in a national assembly of representatives, the origin of the right is the same in all cases. The first, as is before observed, is defective in power; the second, is practicable only in democracies of small extent; the third, is the greatest scale upon which human government can be instituted.

Next to matters of *principle* are matters of *opinion*, and it is necessary to distinguish between the two. Whether the rights of men shall be equal is not a matter of opinion but of right, and consequently of principle; for men do not hold their rights as grants from each other, but each one in right of himself. Society is the guardian but not the giver. And as in extensive societies, such as America and France, the right of the individual in matters of government cannot be exercised but by election and representation, it consequently follows that the only system of government consistent with principle, where simple democracy is impracticable, is the representative system. But as to the organical part, or the manner in which the several parts of government shall be arranged and composed, it is altogether *matter of opinion*, It is necessary that all the parts be conformable with the *principle of equal rights*; and so long as this principle be religiously adhered to, no very material error can take place, neither can any error continue long in that part which falls within the province of opinion.

In all matters of opinion, the social compact, or the principle by which society is held together, requires that the majority of opinions becomes the rule for the whole, and that the minority yields practical obedience thereto. This is perfectly conformable to the principle of equal rights: for, in the first place, every man has a *right to give an opinion* but no man has a right that his opinion should *govern the rest.* In the second place, it is not supposed to be known beforehand on which side of any question, whether for or against, any man's opinion will fall. He may happen to be in a majority upon some questions, and in a minority upon others; and by the same rule that he expects obedience in the one case, he must yield it in the other. All the disorders that have arisen in France, during the progress of the revolution, have had their origin, not in the *principle of equal rights*, but in the violation of that principle. The principle of equal rights has been repeatedly violated, and that not by the majority but by the minority, and *that minority has been composed of men possessing property as well as of men without property; property, therefore, even upon the experience already had, is no more a criterion of character than it is of rights.* It will sometimes happen that the minority are right, and the majority are wrong, but as soon as experience proves this to be the case, the minority will increase to a majority, and the error will reform itself by the tranquil operation of freedom of opinion and equality of rights. Nothing, therefore, can justify an insurrection, neither can it ever be necessary where rights are equal and opinions free.

Taking then the principle of equal rights as the foundation of the revolution, and consequently of the constitution, the organical part, or the manner in which the several parts of the government shall be arranged in the constitution, will, as is already said, fall within the province of opinion.

Various methods will present themselves upon a question of this kind, and though experience is yet wanting to determine which is the best, it has, I think, sufficiently decided which is the worst. That is the worst, which in its deliberations and decisions is subject to the precipitancy and passion of an individual; and when the whole legislature is crowded into one body it is an individual in mass. In all cases of deliberation it is necessary to have a corps of reserve, and it would be better to divide the representation by lot into two parts, and let them revise and correct each other, than that the whole should sit together, and debate at once.

Representative government is not necessarily confined to any one particular form. The principle is the same in all the forms under which it can be arranged. The equal rights of the people is the root from which the whole springs, and the branches may be arranged as present opinion or future experience shall best direct. As to that *hospital of incurables* (as Chesterfield calls it), the British house of peers, it is an excrescence growing out of corruption; and there is no more affinity or resemblance between any of the branches of a legislative body originating from the right of the people, and the aforesaid house of peers, than between a regular member of the human body and an ulcerated wen.

As to that part of government that is called the *executive*, it is necessary in the first place to fix a precise meaning to the word.

There are but two divisions into which power can be arranged. First, that of willing or decreeing the laws; secondly, that of executing or putting them in practice. The former corresponds to the intellectual faculties of the human mind, which reasons and determines what shall be done; the second, to the mechanical powers of the human body, that puts that determination into practice.[17] If the former decides, and the latter does not perform, it is a state of imbecility; and if the latter acts without the predetermination of the former, it is a state of lunacy. The executive department therefore is official, and is subordinate to the legislative, as the body is to the mind, in a state of health; for it is impossible to conceive the idea of two sovereignties, a sovereignty to *will*, and a sovereignty to *act*. The executive is not invested with the power of deliberating whether it shall act or not; it has no discretionary authority in the case; for it can *act no other thing* than what the laws decree, and it is *obliged* to act

[17] Paine may have had in mind the five senses, with reference to the proposed five members of the Directory. —Conway

conformably thereto; and in this view of the case, the executive is made up of all the official departments that execute the laws, of which that which is called the judiciary is the chief.

But mankind have conceived an idea that *some kind of authority* is necessary to *superintend* the execution of the laws and to see that they are faithfully performed; and it is by confounding this superintending authority with the official execution that we get embarrassed about the term *executive power*. All the parts in the governments of the United States of America that are called THE EXECUTIVE, are no other than authorities to superintend the execution of the laws; and they are so far independent of the legislative, that they know the legislative only thro' the laws, and cannot be controlled or directed by it through any other medium.

In what manner this superintending authority shall be appointed, or composed, is a matter that falls within the province of opinion. Some may prefer one method and some another; and in all cases, where opinion only and not principle is concerned, the majority of opinions forms the rule for all. There are however some things deducible from reason, and evidenced by experience, that serve to guide our decision upon the case. The one is, never to invest any individual with extraordinary power; for besides his being tempted to misuse it, it will excite contention and commotion in the nation for the office. Secondly, never to invest power long in the hands of any number of individuals. The inconveniences that may be supposed to accompany frequent changes are less to be feared than the danger that arises from long continuance.

I shall conclude this discourse with offering some observations on the means of *preserving liberty*; for it is not only necessary that we establish it, but that we preserve it.

It is, in the first place, necessary that we distinguish between the means made use of to overthrow despotism, in order to prepare the way for the establishment of liberty, and the means to be used after the despotism is overthrown.

The means made use of in the first case are justified by necessity. Those means are, in general, insurrections; for whilst the established government of despotism continues in any country it is scarcely possible that any other means can be used. It is also certain that in the commencement of a revolution, the revolutionary party permit to themselves a *discretionary exercise of power* regulated more by circumstances than by principle, which, were the practice to continue, liberty would never be established, or if established would soon be overthrown. It is never to be expected in a revolution that every man is to change his opinion at the same moment. There never yet was any truth or any principle so irresistibly obvious, that all men believed it at once. Time and reason must cooperate with each other to the final establishment of any principle; and therefore those who may happen to be first convinced have not a right to persecute others, on whom conviction operates more slowly. The moral principle of revolutions is to instruct, not to destroy.

Had a constitution been established two years ago, (as ought to have been done,) the violences that have since desolated France and injured the character of the revolution, would, in my opinion, have been prevented.[18] The nation would then have had a bond of union, and every individual would have known the line of conduct he was to follow. But, instead of this, a revolutionary government, a thing without either principle or authority, was substituted in its place; virtue and crime depended upon accident; and that which was patriotism one day, became treason the next. All these things have followed from the want of a constitution; for it is the nature and intention of a constitution to *prevent governing by party*, by establishing a common principle that shall limit and control the power and impulse of party, and that says to all parties, *thus far shalt thou go and no further*. But in the absence of a constitution, men look entirely to party; and instead of principle governing party, party governs principle.

An avidity to punish is always dangerous to liberty. It leads men to stretch, to misinterpret, and to misapply even the best of laws. He that would make his own liberty secure, must guard even his enemy from oppression; for if he violates this duty, he establishes a precedent that will reach to himself.

THOMAS PAINE.
Paris, July, 1795.

---

[18] The Constitution adopted August 10, 1793, was by the determination of "The Mountain," suspended during the war against France. The revolutionary government was thus made chronic. —Conway

THE DECLINE AND FALL OF THE ENGLISH SYSTEM OF FINANCE[19]

"On the verge, nay even in the gulf of bankruptcy."
DEBATES IN PARLIAMENT

Nothing, they say, is more certain than death, and nothing more uncertain than the time of dying; yet we can always fix a period beyond which man cannot live, and within some moment of which he will die. We are enabled to do this, not by any spirit of prophecy, or foresight into the event, but by observation of what has happened in all cases of human or animal existence. If then any other subject, such, for instance, as a system of finance, exhibits in its progress a series of symptoms indicating decay, its final dissolution is certain, and the period of it can be calculated from the symptoms it exhibits.

Those who have hitherto written on the English system of finance, (the funding system,) have been uniformly impressed with the idea that its

[19] This pamphlet, as Paine predicts at its close (no doubt on good grounds), was translated into all languages of Europe, and probably hastened the gold suspension of the Bank of England (1797), which it predicted. The British Government entrusted its reply to Ralph Broome and George Chalmers, who wrote pamphlets. There is in the French Archives an order for 1,000 copies, April 27, 1796, nineteen days after Paine's pamphlet appeared.

> "Mr. Cobbett has made this little pamphlet a textbook for most of his elaborate treatises on our finances.... On the authority of a late Register of Mr. Cobbett's I learn that the profits arising from the sale of this pamphlet were devoted [by Paine] to the relief of the prisoners confined in Newgate for debt."
>
> Life of Paine, *by Richard Carlile, 1819*
>
> —Conway

downfall would happen *some time or other*. They took, however, no data for their opinion, but expressed it predictively—or merely as opinion, from a conviction that the perpetual duration of such a system was a natural impossibility. It is in this manner that Dr. Price has spoken of it; and Smith, in his *Wealth of Nations*, has spoken in the same manner; that is, merely as opinion without data. "The progress," says Smith, "of the enormous debts, which at present oppress, and will in the long run *most probably ruin*, all the great nations of Europe [he should have said *governments*] has been pretty uniform." But this general manner of speaking, though it might make some impression, carried with it no conviction.

It is not my intention to predict anything; but I will show from data already known, from symptoms and facts which the English funding system has already exhibited publicly, that it will not continue to the end of Mr. Pitt's life, supposing him to live the usual age of a man. How much sooner it may fall, I leave to others to predict.

Let financiers diversify systems of credit as they will, it *is* nevertheless true, that every system of credit is a system of paper money. Two experiments have already been had upon paper money; the one in America, the other in France. In both those cases the whole capital was emitted, and that whole capital, which in America was called continental money, and in France assignats, appeared in circulation; the consequence of which was, that the quantity became so enormous, and so disproportioned to the quantity of population, and to the quantity of objects upon which it could be employed, that the market, if I may so express it, was glutted with it, and the value of it fell. Between five and six years determined the fate of those experiments. The same fate would have happened to gold and silver, could gold and silver have been issued in the same abundant manner that paper had been, and confined within the country as paper money always is, by having no circulation out of it; or, to speak on a larger scale, the same thing would happen in the world, could the world be glutted with gold and silver, as America and France have been with paper.

The English system differs from that of America and France in this one particular, that its capital is kept out of sight; that is, it does not appear in circulation. Were the whole capital of the national debt, which at the time I write this is almost one hundred million pounds sterling, to be emitted in assignats or bills, and that whole quantity put into circulation, as was done in America and in France, those English assignats, or bills, would soon sink in value as those of America and France have done; and that in a greater degree, because the quantity of them would be more disproportioned to the quantity of population in England, than was the case in either of the other two countries. A nominal pound sterling in such bills would not be worth one penny.

But though the English system, by thus keeping the capital out of sight, is preserved from hasty destruction, as in the case of America and France, it nevertheless approaches the same fate, and will arrive at it with the same certainty, though by a slower progress. The difference is altogether in the degree of speed by which the two systems approach their fate, which, to speak in round numbers, is as twenty is to one; that is, the English system, that of funding the capital instead of issuing it, contained within itself a capacity of enduring twenty times longer than the systems adopted by America and France; and at the end of that time it would arrive at the same common grave, the Potter's Field of paper money.

The datum, I take for this proportion of twenty to one, is the difference between a capital and the interest at five percent. Twenty times the interest is equal to the capital. The accumulation of paper money in England is in proportion to the accumulation of the interest upon every new loan; and therefore the progress to the dissolution is twenty times slower than if the capital were to be emitted and put into circulation immediately. Every twenty years in the English system is equal to one year in the French and American systems.

Having thus stated the duration of the two systems, that of funding upon interest, and that of emitting the whole capital without funding, to be as twenty to one, I come to examine the symptoms of decay, approaching to dissolution, that the English system has already exhibited, and to compare them with similar systems in the French and American systems.

The English funding system began one hundred years ago; in which time there have been six wars, including the war that ended in 1697.

1. The war that ended, as I have just said, in 1697.
2. The war that began in 1702.
3. The war that began in 1739.
4. The war that began in 1756.
5. The American war, that began in 1775.
6. The present war, that began in 1793.

The national debt, at the conclusion of the war which ended in 1697, was twenty-one millions and an half. (See Smith's *Wealth of Nations*, chapter on Public Debts.) We now see it approaching fast to four hundred millions. If between these two extremes of twenty-one millions and four hundred millions, embracing the several expenses of all the including wars, there exist some common ratio that will ascertain arithmetically the amount of the debts at the end of each war, as certainly as the fact is known to be, that ratio will in like manner determine what the amount of the debt will be in all future wars, and will ascertain the period within which the funding system will expire in a bankruptcy of the government; for the ratio I allude to, is the ratio which the nature of the thing has established for itself.

Hitherto no idea has been entertained that any such ratio existed, or could exist, that would determine a problem of this kind; that is, that would ascertain, without having any knowledge of the fact, what the expense of any former war had been, or what the expense of any future war would be; but it is nevertheless true that such a ratio does exist, as I shall show, and also the mode of applying it.

The ratio I allude to is not in arithmetical progression like the numbers 2, 3, 4, 5, 6, 7, 8, 9; nor yet in geometrical progression, like the numbers 2, 4, 8, 16, 32, 64, 128, 256; but it is in the series of one half upon each preceding number; like the numbers 8, 12, 18, 27, 40, 60, 90, 135.

Any person can perceive that the second number, 12, is produced by the preceding number, 8, and half 8; and that the third number, 18, is in like manner produced by the preceding number, 12, and half 12; and so on for the rest. They can also see how rapidly the sums increase as the ratio proceeds. The difference between the two first numbers is but four; but the difference between the two last is forty-five; and from thence they may see with what immense rapidity the national debt has increased, and will continue to increase, till it exceeds the ordinary powers of calculation, and loses itself in ciphers.

I come now to apply the ratio as a rule to determine in all cases.

I began with the war that ended in 1697, which was the war in which the funding system began. The expense of that war was twenty-one millions and an half. In order to ascertain the expense of the next war, I add to twenty-one millions and an half, the half thereof (ten millions and three quarters) which makes thirty-two millions and a quarter for the expense of that war. This thirty-two millions and a quarter, added to the former debt of twenty-one millions and an half, carries the national debt to fifty-three millions and three quarters. Smith, in his chapter on Public Debts, says, that the national debt was at this time fifty-three millions.

I proceed to ascertain the expense of the next war, that of 1739, by adding, as in the former case, one half to the expense of the preceding war. The expense of the preceding war was thirty-two millions and a quarter; for the sake of even numbers, say, thirty-two millions; the half of which (sixteen) makes forty-eight millions for the expense of that war.

I proceed to ascertain the expense of the war of 1756, by adding, according to the ratio, one half to the expense of the preceding war. The expense of the preceding was taken at forty-eight millions, the half of which (twenty-four) makes seventy-two millions for the expense of that war. Smith, (chapter on Public Debts,) says, the expense of the war of 1756, was seventy-two millions and a quarter.

I proceed to ascertain the expense of the American war, of 1775, by adding, as in the former cases, one half to the expense of the preceding war. The expense of the preceding war was seventy-two millions, the half of which (thirty-six) makes 108 millions for the expense of that war. In the last edition of Smith, (chapter on Public Debts,) he says, the expense of the American war was *more than an hundred millions*.

I come now to ascertain the expense of the present war, supposing it to continue as long as former wars have done, and the funding system not to break up before that period. The expense of the preceding war was 108 millions, the half of which (fifty-four) makes 162 millions for the expense of the present war. It gives symptoms of going beyond this sum, supposing the funding system not to break up; for the loans of the last year and of the present year are twenty-two millions each, which exceeds the ratio compared with the loans of the preceding war. It will not be from the inability of procuring loans that the system will break up. On the contrary, it is the facility with which loans can be procured that hastens that event. The loans are altogether paper transactions; and it is the excess of them that brings on, with accelerating speed, that progressive depreciation of funded paper money that will dissolve the funding system.

I proceed to ascertain the expense of future wars, and I do this merely to show the impossibility of the continuance of the funding system, and the certainty of its dissolution.

The expense of the next war after the present war, according to the ratio that has ascertained the preceding cases, will be

War		*Expense (£)*	
		243	millions.
Expense of the	second war	364	
"	third war	546	
"	fourth war	819	
"	fifth war	1,228	
		£3,200	millions;

which, at only four percent will require taxes to the nominal amount of one hundred and twenty-eight millions to pay the annual interest, besides the interest of the present debt, and the expenses of government, which are not included in this account. Is there a man so mad, so stupid, as to suppose this system can continue?

When I first conceived the idea of seeking for some common ratio that should apply as a rule of measurement to all the cases of the funding system, so far as to ascertain the several stages of its approach to dissolution, I had no expectation that any ratio could be found that would apply with so much exactness as this does. I was led to the idea merely by observing that the funding system was a thing in continual progression, and that whatever was in a state of progression might be supposed to admit of, at least, some general ratio of measurement, that would apply without any very great variation. But who could have supposed that falling systems, or falling opinions, admitted of a ratio apparently as true as the descent of falling bodies? I have not made the ratio any more than Newton made the ratio of gravitation. I have only discovered it, and explained the mode of applying it.

To show at one view the rapid progression of the funding system to destruction, and to expose the folly of those who blindly believe in its continuance, and who artfully endeavour to impose that belief upon others, I exhibit in the annexed table, the expense of each of the six wars since the funding system began, as ascertained by ratio, and the expense of the six wars yet to come, ascertained by the same ratio.

First six wars			Second six wars		
War	*Expense (£)*		*War*	*Expense (£)*	
1.	21	millions	1.	243	millions
2.	33	"	2.	364	"
3.	48	"	3.	546	"
4.	72	"See note	4.	819	"
5.	108	"	5.	1,228	"
6.	162	"	6.	1,842	"
Total	£444	"	Total	£5,042	"

Note: The actual expense of the war of 1739 did not come up to the sum ascertained by the ratio. But as that which is the natural disposition of a thing, as it is the natural disposition of a stream of water to descend, will, if impeded in its course, overcome by a new effort what it had lost by that impediment, so it was with respect to this war and the next (1756) taken collectively; for the expense of the war of 1756 restored the equilibrium of the ratio, as fully as if it had not been impeded. A circumstance that serves to prove the truth of the ratio more folly than if the interruption had not taken place. The war of 1739 was languid; the efforts were below the value of money et that time; for the ratio is the measure of the depreciation of money in consequence of the funding system; or what comes to the same end, it is the measure of the increase of paper. Every additional quantity of it, whether in bank notes or otherwise, diminishes the real, though not the nominal value of the former quantity.

Those who are acquainted with the power with which even a small ratio, acting in progression, multiplies in a long series, will see nothing to wonder at in this table. Those who are not acquainted with that subject, and not knowing what else to say, may be inclined to deny it. But it is not their opinion one way, nor mine the other, that can influence the event. The table exhibits the natural march of the funding system to its irredeemable dissolution. Supposing the present government of England to continue, and to go on as it has gone on since the funding system began, I would not give twenty shillings for one hundred pounds in the funds to be paid twenty years hence. I do not speak this predictively; I produce the data upon which that belief is founded; and which data it is everybody's interest to know, who have anything to do with the funds, or who are going to bequeath property to their descendants to be paid at a future day.

Perhaps it may be asked, that as governments or ministers proceeded by no ratio in making loans or incurring debts, and nobody intended any ratio, or thought of any, how does it happen that there is one? I answer, that the ratio is founded in necessity; and I now go to explain what that necessity is.

It will always happen, that the price of labour, or of the produce of labour, be that produce what it may, will be in proportion to the quantity of money in a country, admitting things to take their natural course. Before the invention of the funding system, there was no other money than gold and silver; and as nature gives out those metals with a sparing hand, and in regular annual quantities from the mines, the several prices of things were proportioned to the quantity of money at that time, and so nearly stationary as to vary but little in any fifty or sixty years of that period.

When the funding system began, a substitute for gold and silver began also. That substitute was paper; and the quantity increased as the quantity of interest increased upon accumulated loans. This appearance of a new and additional species of money in the nation soon began to break the relative value which money and the things it will purchase bore to each other before. Everything rose in price; but the rise at first was little and slow, like the difference in units between two first numbers, 8 and 12, compared with the two last numbers 90 and 135, in the table. It was however sufficient to make itself considerably felt in a large transaction. When therefore government, by engaging in a new war, required a new loan, it was obliged to make a higher loan than the former loan, to balance the increased price to which things had risen; and as that new loan increased the quantity of paper in proportion to the new quantity of interest, it carried the price of things still higher than before. The next loan was again higher, to balance that further increased price; and all this in the same manner, though not in the same degree, that every new emission of continental money in America, or of assignats in France, was greater than the preceding emission, to make head against the advance of prices, till the combat could be maintained no longer. Herein is founded the necessity of which I have just spoken. That necessity proceeds with accelerating velocity, and the ratio I have laid down is the measure of that acceleration; or, to speak the technical language of the subject, it is the measure of the increasing depreciation of funded paper money, which it is impossible to prevent while the quantity of that money and of bank notes continues to multiply. What else but this can account for the difference between one war costing twenty-one millions, and another war costing 160 millions?

The difference cannot be accounted for on the score of extraordinary efforts or extraordinary achievements. The war that cost twenty-one millions was the war of the confederates, historically called the grand alliance, consisting of England, Austria, and Holland in the time of William III against Louis XIV and in which the confederates were victorious. The present is a war of a much greater confederacy—a confederacy of England, Austria, Prussia, the German Empire, Spain, Holland, Naples, and Sardinia, eight powers, against the French Republic singly, and the Republic has beaten the whole confederacy.—But to return to my subject.

It is said in England, that the value of paper keeps equal with the value of gold and silver. But the case is not rightly stated; for the fact is, that the paper has *pulled down* the value of gold and silver to a level with itself. Gold and silver will not purchase so much of any purchasable article at this day as if no paper had appeared, nor so much as it will in any country in Europe where there is no paper. How long this hanging together of money and paper will continue, makes a new case; because it daily exposes the system to sudden death, independent of the natural death it would otherwise suffer.

I consider the funding system as being now advanced into the last twenty years of its existence. The single circumstance, were there no other, that a war should now cost nominally one hundred and sixty millions, which when the system began cost but twenty-one millions, or that the loan for one year only (including the loan to the Emperor) should now be nominally greater than the whole expense of that war, shows the state of depreciation to which the funding system has arrived. Its depreciation is in the proportion of eight for one, compared with the value of its money when the system began; which is the state the French assignats stood a year ago (March 1795) compared with gold and silver. It is therefore that I say, that the English funding system has entered on the last twenty years of its existence, comparing each twenty years of the English system with every single year of the American and French systems, as before stated.

Again, supposing the present war to close as former wars have done, and without producing either revolution or reform in England, another war at least must be looked for in the space of the twenty years I allude to;

for it has never yet happened that twenty years have passed off without a war, and that more especially since the English government has dabbled in German politics, and shown a disposition to insult the world, and the world of commerce, with her navy. The next war will carry the national debt to very nearly seven hundred millions, the interest of which, at four percent, will be twenty-eight millions besides the taxes for the (then) expenses of government, which will increase in the same proportion, and which will carry the taxes to at least forty millions; and if another war only begins, it will quickly carry them to above fifty; for it is in the last twenty years of the funding system, as in the last year of the American and French systems without funding, that all the great shocks begin to operate.

I have just mentioned that, paper in England has *pulled down* the value of gold and silver to a level with itself; and that *this pulling dawn* of gold and silver money has created the appearance of paper money keeping up. The same thing, and the same mistake, took place in America and in France, and continued for a considerable time after the commencement of their system of paper; and the actual depreciation of money was hidden under that mistake.

It was said in America, at that time, that everything was becoming *dear*; but gold and silver could then buy those dear articles no cheaper than paper could; and therefore it was not called depreciation. The idea of *dearness* established itself for the idea of depreciation. The same was the case in France. Though everything rose in price soon after assignats appeared, yet those dear articles could be purchased no cheaper with gold and silver, than with paper, and it was only said that things were *dear*. The same is still the language in England. They call it *deariness*. But they will soon find that it is an actual depreciation, and that this depreciation is the effect of the funding system; which, by crowding such a continually increasing mass of paper into circulation, carries down the value of gold and silver with it. But gold and silver, will, in the long run, revolt against depreciation, and separate from the value of paper; for the progress of all such systems appears to be, that the paper will take the command in the beginning, and gold and silver in the end.

But this succession in the command of gold and silver over paper, makes a crisis far more eventful to the funding system than to any other system upon which paper can be issued; for, strictly speaking, it is not a crisis of danger but a symptom of death. It is a death-stroke to the funding system. It is a revolution in the whole of its affairs.

If paper be issued without being funded upon interest, emissions of it can be continued after the value of it separates from gold and silver, as we have seen in the two cases of America and France. But the funding system rests altogether upon the value of paper being equal to gold and silver; which will be as long as the paper can continue carrying down the value of gold and silver to the same level to which itself descends, and no longer. But even in this state, that of descending equally together, the minister, whoever he may be, will find himself beset with accumulating difficulties; because the loans and taxes voted for the service of each ensuing year will wither in his hands before the year expires, or before they can be applied. This will force him to have recourse to emissions of what are called exchequer and navy bills, which, by still increasing the mass of paper in circulation, will drive on the depreciation still more rapidly.

It ought to be known that taxes in England are not paid in gold and silver, but in paper (bank notes). Every person who pays any considerable quantity of taxes, such as maltsters, brewers, distillers, (I appeal for the truth of it, to any of the collectors of excise in England, or to Mr. Whitbread,)[20] knows this to be the case. There is not gold and silver enough in the nation to pay the taxes in coin, as I shall show; and consequently there is not money enough in the bank to pay the notes. The interest of the national funded debt is paid at the bank in the same kind of paper in which the taxes are collected. When people find, as they will find, a reservedness among each other in giving gold and silver for bank notes, or the least preference for the former over the latter, they will go for payment to the bank, where they have a right to go. They will do this as a measure of prudence, each one for himself, and the truth or delusion of the funding system will then be proved.

I have said in the foregoing paragraph that there is not gold and silver enough in the nation to pay the taxes in coin, and consequently that there cannot be enough in the bank to pay the notes. As I do not choose to rest anything upon assertion, I appeal for the truth of this to the publications of Mr. Eden (now called Lord Auckland) and George Chalmers, Secretary to the Board of Trade and Plantation, of which

[20] An eminent Member of Parliament. —Conway

Jenkinson (now Lord Hawkesbury) is president.[21] (These sort of folks change their names so often that it is as difficult to know them as it is to know a thief.) Chalmers gives the quantity of gold and silver coin from the returns of coinage at the Mint; and after deducting for the light gold recoined, says that the amount of gold and silver coined is about twenty millions. He had better not have proved this, especially if he had reflected that *public credit is suspicion asleep*. The quantity is much too little.

Of this twenty millions (which is not a fourth part of the quantity of gold and silver there is in France, as is shown in Mr. Neckar's *Treatise on the Administration of the Finances*) three millions at least must be supposed to be in Ireland, some in Scotland, and in the West Indies, Newfoundland, etc. The quantity therefore in England cannot be more than sixteen millions, which is four millions less than the amount of the taxes. But admitting that there are sixteen millions, not more than a fourth part thereof (four millions) can be in London, when it is considered that every city, town, village, and farmhouse in the nation must have a part of it, and that all the great manufactories, which most require cash, are out of London. Of this four millions in London, every banker, merchant, tradesman, in short every individual, must have some. He must be a poor shopkeeper indeed, who has not a few guineas in his till. The quantity of cash therefore in the bank can never, on the evidence of circumstances, be so much as two millions; most probably not more than one million; and on this slender twig, always liable to be broken, hangs the whole funding system of four hundred millions, besides many millions in bank notes. The sum in the bank is not sufficient to pay one-fourth of only one year's interest of the national debt, were the creditors to demand payment in cash, or demand cash for the bank notes in which the interest is paid, a circumstance always liable to happen.

One of the amusements that has kept up the farce of the funding system is, that the interest is regularly paid. But as the interest is always paid in bank notes, and as bank notes can always be coined for the purpose, this mode of payment proves nothing. The point of proof is, can the bank give cash for the bank notes with which the interest is paid? If it cannot, and it is evident it cannot, some millions of bank notes must go without payment, and those holders of bank notes who apply last

[21] Concerning Chalmers and Hawkesbury see my appendix to *The Rights of Man*. Also, preface to my *Life of Paine*, xvi, and other passages. —Conway

will be worst off. When the present quantity of cash in the bank is paid away, it is next to impossible to see how any new quantity is to arrive. None will arrive from taxes, for the taxes will all be paid in bank notes; and should the government refuse bank notes in payment of taxes, the credit of bank notes will be gone at once. No cash will arise from the business of discounting merchants' bills; for every merchant will pay off those bills in bank notes, and not in cash. There is therefore no means left for the bank to obtain a new supply of cash, after the present quantity is paid away. But besides the impossibility of paying the interest of the funded debt in cash, there are many thousand persons, in London and in the country, who are holders of bank notes that came into their hands in the fair way of trade, and who are not stockholders in the funds; and as such persons have had no hand in increasing the demand upon the bank, as those have had who for their own private interest, like Boyd and others, are contracting or pretending to contract for new loans, they will conceive they have a just right that their bank notes should be paid first. Boyd has been very sly in France, in changing his paper into cash. He will be just as sly in doing the same thing in London, for he has learned to calculate; and then it is probable he will set off for America.

A stoppage of payment at the bank is not a new thing. Smith in his *Wealth of Nations*, book ii chap. 2, says, that in the year 1696, exchequer bills fell forty, fifty, and sixty percent; bank notes twenty percent; and the bank stopped payment. That which happened in 1696 may happen again in 1796. The period in which it happened was the last year of the war of King William. It necessarily put a stop to the further emissions of exchequer and navy bills, and to the raising of new loans; and the peace which took place the next year was probably hurried on by this circumstance, and saved the bank from bankruptcy. Smith in speaking from the circumstances of the bank, upon another occasion, says (book ii chap. 2) "This great company had been reduced to the necessity of paying in sixpences." When a bank adopts the expedient of paying in sixpences, it is a confession of insolvency.

It is worthy of observation, that every case of failure in finances, since the system of paper began, has produced a revolution in governments, either total or partial. A failure in the finances of France produced the French revolution. A failure in the finance of the assignats broke up the revolutionary government, and produced the present French Constitution. A failure in the finances of the Old Congress of America, and the embarrassments it brought upon commerce, broke up the system of the old confederation, and produced the federal Constitution. If, then, we admit of reasoning by comparison of causes and events, the failure of the English finances will produce some change in the government of that country.

As to Mr. Pitt's project of paying off the national debt by applying a million a-year for that purpose, while he continues adding more than twenty millions a-year to it, it is like setting a man with a wooden leg to run after a hare. The longer he runs the farther he is off.

When I said that the funding system had entered the last twenty years of its existence, I certainly did not mean that it would continue twenty years, and then expire as a lease would do. I meant to describe that age of decrepitude in which death is every day to be expected, and life cannot continue long. But the death of credit, or that state that is called bankruptcy, is not always marked by those progressive stages of visible decline that marked the decline of natural life. In the progression of natural life age cannot counterfeit youth, nor conceal the departure of juvenile abilities. But it is otherwise with respect to the death of credit; for though all the approaches to bankruptcy may actually exist in circumstances, they admit of being concealed by appearances. Nothing is more common than to see the bankrupt of today a man in credit but the day before; yet no sooner is the real state of his affairs known, than everybody can see he had been insolvent long before. In London, the greatest theatre of bankruptcy in Europe, this part of the subject will be well and feelingly understood.

Mr. Pitt continually talks of credit, and the national resources. These are two of the feigned appearances by which the approaches to bankruptcy are concealed. That which he calls credit may exist, as I have just shown, in a state of insolvency, and is always what I have before described it to be, *suspicion asleep*.

As to national resources, Mr. Pitt, like all English financiers that preceded him since the funding system began, has uniformly mistaken the nature of a resource; that is, they have mistaken it consistently with the delusion of the funding system; but time is explaining the delusion. That which he calls, and which they call, a resource, is not a resource, but is the *anticipation* of a resource. They have anticipated what *would have been* a resource in another generation, had not the use of it been so anticipated. The funding system is a system of anticipation. Those who established it an hundred years ago anticipated the resources of those who were to live an hundred years after; for the people of the present day have to pay the interest of the debts contracted at that time, and all debts contracted since. But it is the last feather that breaks the horse's back. Had the system begun an hundred years before, the amount of taxes at this time to pay the annual interest at four percent (could we suppose such a system of insanity could have continued) would be two hundred and twenty millions annually: for the capital of the debt would be 5,486 millions, according to the ratio that ascertains the expense of the wars for the hundred years that are past. But long before it could have reached this period, the value of bank notes, from the immense quantity of them, (for it is in paper only that such a nominal revenue could be collected,) would have been as low or lower than continental paper has been in America, or assignats in France; and as to the idea of exchanging them for gold and silver, it is too absurd to be contradicted.

Do we not see that nature, in all her operations, disowns the visionary basis upon which the funding system is built? She acts always by renewed successions, and never by accumulating additions perpetually progressing. Animals and vegetables, men and trees, have existed since the world began: but that existence has been carried on by succession of generations, and not by continuing the same men and the same trees in existence that existed first; and to make room for the new she removes the old. Every natural idiot can see this; it is the stock-jobbing idiot only that mistakes. He has conceived that art can do what nature cannot. He is teaching her a new system—that there is no occasion for man to die—that the scheme of creation can be carried on upon the plan of the funding system—that it can proceed by continual additions of new beings, like new loans, and all live together in eternal youth. Go, count the graves, thou idiot, and learn the folly of thy arithmetic!

But besides these things, there is something visibly farcical in the whole operation of loaning. It is scarcely more than four years ago that such a rot of bankruptcy spread itself over London, that the whole commercial fabric tottered; trade and credit were at a stand; and such was the state of things that, to prevent or suspend a general bankruptcy, the government lent the merchants six millions in *government* paper, and now the merchants lend the government twenty-two millions in *their* paper; and two parties, Boyd and Morgan, men but little known, contend who shall be the lenders. What a farce is this! It reduces the operation of loaning to accommodation paper, in which the competitors contend, not who shall lend, but who shall sign, because there is something to be got for signing.

Every English stockjobber and minister boasts of the credit of England. Its credit, say they, is greater than that of any country in Europe. There is a good reason for this: for there is not another country in Europe that could be made the dupe of such a delusion. The English funding system will remain a monument of wonder, not so much on account of the extent to which it has been carried, as of the folly of believing in it.

Those who had formerly predicted that the funding system would break up when the debt should amount to one hundred or one hundred and fifty millions, erred only in not distinguishing between insolvency and actual bankruptcy; for the insolvency commenced as soon as the government became unable to pay the interest in cash, or to give cash for the bank notes in which the interest was paid, whether that inability was known or not, or whether it was suspected or not. Insolvency always takes place before bankruptcy; for bankruptcy is nothing more than the publication of that insolvency. In the affairs of an individual, it often happens that insolvency exists several years before bankruptcy, and that the insolvency is concealed and carried on till the individual is not able to pay one shilling in the pound. A government can ward off bankruptcy longer than an individual: but insolvency will inevitably produce bankruptcy, whether in an individual or in a government. If then the quantity of bank notes payable on demand, which the bank has issued, are greater than the bank can pay off, the bank is insolvent: and when that insolvency is declared, it is bankruptcy.[22]

---

[22] Among the delusions that have been imposed upon the nation by ministers to give a false colouring to its affairs, and by none more than by Mr. Pitt, is a motley, amphibious-charactered thing called the *balance of trade*. This balance of trade, as it is called, is taken from the customhouse books, in which entries are made of all cargoes exported, and also of all cargoes imported, in each year; and when the value of the exports, according to the price set upon them by the exporter or by the customhouse, is greater than the value of the imports, estimated in the same manner, they say the balance of trade is much in their favour.

The customhouse books prove regularly enough that so many cargoes have been exported, and so many imported; but this is all that they prove, or were intended to prove. They have nothing to do with the balance of profit or loss; and it is ignorance to appeal to them upon that account: for the case is, that the greater the loss is in any

I come now to show the several ways by which bank notes get into circulation: I shall afterwards offer an estimate on the total quantity or amount of bank notes existing at this moment.

The bank acts in three capacities. As a bank of discount; as a bank of deposit; and as a banker for the government.

First, as a bank of discount. The bank discounts merchants' bills of exchange for two months. When a merchant has a bill that will become due at the end of two months, and wants payment before that time, the bank advances that payment to him, deducting therefrom at the rate of five percent per annum. The bill of exchange remains at the bank as a pledge or pawn, and at the end of two months it must be redeemed. This transaction is done altogether in paper; for the profits of the bank, as a bank of discount, arise entirely from its making use of paper as money. The bank gives bank notes to the merchant in discounting the bill of exchange, and the redeemer of the bill pays bank notes to the bank in redeeming it. It very seldom happens that any real money passes between them.

If the profits of a bank be, for example, two hundred thousand pounds a year (a great sum to be made merely by exchanging one sort of paper for another, and which shows also that the merchants of that place are pressed for money for payments, instead of having money to spare to lend to government,) it proves that the bank discounts to the amount

---

one year, the higher will this thing called the balance of trade appear to be according to the customhouse books. For example, nearly the whole of the Mediterranean convoy has been taken by the French this year; consequently those cargoes will not appear as imports on the customhouse books, and therefore the balance of trade, by which they mean the profits of it, will appear to be so much the greater as the loss amounts to; and, on the other hand, had the loss not happened, the profits would have appeared to have been so much the less. All the losses happening at sea to returning cargoes, by accidents, by the elements, or by capture, make the balance appear the higher on the side of the exports; and were they all lost at sea, it would appear to be all profit on the customhouse books. Also every cargo of exports that is lost that occasions another to be sent, adds in like manner to the side of the exports, and appears as profit. This year the balance of trade will appear high, because the losses have been great by capture and by storms. The ignorance of the British Parliament in listening to this hackneyed imposition of ministers about the balance of trade is astonishing. It shows how little they know of national affairs—and Mr. Grey may as well talk Greek to them, as to make motions about the state of the nation. They understand only foxhunting and the game laws.

of four millions annually, or £666,666 every two months; and as there never remain in the bank more than two months' pledges, of the value of £666,666, at any one time, the amount of bank notes in circulation at any one time should not be more than to that amount. This is sufficient to show that the present immense quantity of bank notes, which are distributed through every city, town, village, and farmhouse in England, cannot be accounted for on the score of discounting.

Secondly, as a bank of deposit. To deposit money at the bank means to lodge it there for the sake of convenience, and to be drawn out at any moment the depositor pleases, or to be paid away to his order. When the business of discounting is great, that of depositing is necessarily small. No man deposits and applies for discounts at the same time; for it would be like paying interest for lending money, instead of for borrowing it. The deposits that are now made at the bank are almost entirely in bank notes, and consequently they add nothing to the ability of the bank to pay off the bank notes that may be presented for payment; and besides this, the deposits are no more the property of the bank than the cash or bank notes in a merchant's countinghouse are the property of his bookkeeper. No great increase therefore of bank notes, beyond what the discounting business admits, can be accounted for on the score of deposits.

Thirdly, the bank acts as banker for the government. This is the connection that threatens to ruin every public bank. It is through this connection that the credit of a bank is forced far beyond what it ought to be, and still further beyond its ability to pay. It is through this connection, that such an immense redundant quantity of bank notes, have gotten into circulation; and which, instead of being issued because there was property in the bank, have been issued because there was none.

When the treasury is empty, which happens in almost every year of every war, its coffers at the bank are empty also. It is in this condition of emptiness that the minister has recourse to emissions of what are called exchequer and navy bills, which continually generates a new increase of bank notes, and which are sported upon the public, without there being property in the bank to pay them. These exchequer and navy bills (being, as I have said, emitted because the treasury and its coffers at the bank are empty, and cannot pay the demands that come in) are no other than an acknowledgment that the bearer is entitled to receive so much money. They may be compared to the settlement of an account, in which the debtor acknowledges the balance he owes, and for which he gives a note of hand; or to a note of hand given to raise money upon it.

Sometimes the bank discounts those bills as it would discount merchants' bills of exchange; sometimes it purchases them of the holders at the current price; and sometimes it agrees with the ministers to pay an interest upon them to the holders, and keep them in circulation. In every one of these cases an additional quantity of bank notes gets into circulation, and are sported, as I have said, upon the public, without there being property in the bank, as banker for the government, to pay them; and besides this, the bank has now no money of its own; for the money that was originally subscribed to begin the credit of the bank with, at its first establishment, has been lent to government and wasted long ago.

"The bank" (says Smith, book ii chap. 2) "acts not only as an ordinary bank, but as a great engine of State; it receives and pays a greater part of the annuities which are due to the creditors of the *public*." (It is worth observing, that the *public*, or the *nation*, is always put for the government, in speaking of debts.) "It circulates" (says Smith) "exchequer bills, and it advances to government the annual amount of the land and malt taxes, which are frequently not paid till several years afterwards." (This advancement is also done in bank notes, for which there is not property in the bank.) "In those different operations" (says Smith) "*its duty to the public* may sometimes have obliged it, without any fault of its directors, *to overstock the circulation with paper money*."—bank notes. How its *duty* to *the public* can induce it *to overstock that public* with promissory bank notes which it *cannot pay*, and thereby expose the individuals of that public to ruin, is too paradoxical to be explained; for it is on the credit which individuals *give to the bank*, by receiving and circulating its notes, and not upon its *own* credit or its *own* property, for it has none, that the bank sports. If, however, it be the duty of the bank to expose the public to this hazard, it is at least equally the duty of the individuals of that public to get their money and take care of themselves; and leave it to placemen, pensioners, government contractors, Reeves' association, and the members of both houses of Parliament, who have voted away the money at the nod of the minister, to continue the credit if they can, and for which their estates individually and collectively ought to answer, as far as they will go.

There has always existed, and still exists, a mysterious, suspicious connection, between the minister and the directors of the bank, and which explains itself no otherways than by a continual increase in bank notes. Without, therefore, entering into any further details of the various contrivances by which bank notes are issued, and thrown upon the public, I proceed, as I before mentioned, to offer an estimate on the total quantity of bank notes in circulation.

However disposed governments may be to wring money by taxes from the people, there is a limit to the practice established by the nature of things. That limit is the proportion between the quantity of money in a nation, be that quantity what it may, and the greatest quantity of taxes that can be raised upon it. People have other uses for money besides paying taxes; and it is only a proportional part of the money they can spare for taxes, as it is only a proportional part they can spare for house-rent, for clothing, or for any other particular use. These proportions find out and establish themselves; and that with such exactness, that if any one part exceeds its proportion, all the other parts feel it.

Before the invention of paper money (bank notes,) there was no other money in the nation than gold and silver, and the greatest quantity of money that was ever raised in taxes during that period never exceeded a fourth part of the quantity of money in the nation. It was high taxing when it came to this point. The taxes in the time of William III never reached to four millions before the invention of paper, and the quantity of money in the nation at that time was estimated to be about sixteen millions. The same proportions established themselves in France. There was no paper money in France before the present revolution, and the taxes were collected in gold and silver money. The highest quantity of taxes never exceeded twenty-two millions sterling; and the quantity of gold and silver money in the nation at the same time, as stated by M. Neckar, from returns of coinage at the Mint, in his *Treatise on the Administration of the Finances*, was about ninety millions sterling. To go beyond this limit of a fourth part, in England, they were obliged to introduce paper money; and the attempt to go beyond it in France, where paper could not be introduced, broke up the government. This proportion, therefore, of a fourth part, is the limit which the thing establishes for itself, be the quantity of money in a nation more or less.

The amount of taxes in England at this time is full twenty millions; and therefore the quantity of gold and silver, and of bank notes, taken together, amounts to eighty millions. The quantity of gold and silver, as stated by Lord Hawkesbury's Secretary, George Chalmers, as I have before shown, is twenty millions; and, therefore, the total amount of bank notes in circulation, all made payable on demand, is sixty millions. This enormous sum will astonish the most stupid stockjobber, and overpower the credulity of the most thoughtless Englishman: but were it only a third part of that sum, the bank cannot pay half a crown in the pound.

There is something curious in the movements of this modern complicated machine, the funding system; and it is only now that it is beginning to unfold the full extent of its movements. In the first part of its movements it gives great powers into the hands of government, and in the last part it takes them completely away.

The funding system set out with raising revenues under the name of loans, by means of which government became both prodigal and powerful. The loaners assumed the name of creditors, and though it was soon discovered that loaning was government-jobbing, those pretended loaners, or the persons who purchased into the funds afterwards, conceived themselves not only to be creditors, but to be the *only* creditors.

But such has been the operation of this complicated machine, the funding system, that it has produced, unperceived, a second generation of creditors, more numerous and far more formidable and withal more real than the first generation; for every holder of a bank note is a creditor, and a real creditor, and the debt due to him is made payable on demand. The debt therefore which the government owes to individuals is composed of two parts; the one about four hundred millions bearing interest, the other about sixty millions payable on demand. The one is called the funded debt, the other is the debt due in bank notes.

The second debt (that contained in the bank notes) has, in a great measure, been incurred to pay the interest of the first debt; so that in fact little or no real interest has been paid by government. The whole has been delusion and fraud. Government first contracted a debt, in the form of loans, with one class of people, and then run clandestinely into debt with another class, by means of bank notes, to pay the interest. Government acted of itself in contracting the first debt, and made a machine of the bank to contract the second. It is this second debt that changes the seat of power and the order of things; for it puts it in the power of even a small part of the holders of bank notes (had they no other motives than disgust at Pitt and Grenville's sedition bills,) to control any measure of government they found to be injurious to their interest; and that not by popular meetings, or popular societies, but by the simple and easy operation of withholding their credit from that government; that is, by individually demanding payment at the bank for every bank note that comes into their hands. Why should Pitt and Grenville expect that the very men whom they insult and injure, should, at the same time, continue to support the measures of Pitt and Grenville, by giving credit to their promissory notes of payment? No new emissions of bank notes could go on while payment was demanding on the old, and the cash in the bank wasting daily away; nor any new advances be made to government, or to the emperor, to carry on the war; nor any new emission be made on exchequer bills.

"The bank," says Smith, (book ii chap. 2) "is a great engine of state." And in the same paragraph he says, "The stability of the bank is equal to that of the British government;" which is the same as to say that the stability of the government is equal to that of the bank, and no more. If then the bank cannot pay, the *arch-treasurer* of the holy Roman empire (S.R.I.A.)[23] is a bankrupt. When Folly invented titles, she did not attend to their application; for ever since the government of England has been in the hands of *arch-treasurers*, it has been running into bankruptcy; and as to the arch-treasurer *apparent*, he has been a bankrupt long ago. What a miserable prospect has England before its eyes!

Before the war of 1755 there were no bank notes lower than twenty pounds. During that war, bank notes of fifteen pounds and of ten pounds were coined; and now, since the commencement of the present war, they are coined as low as five pounds. These five-pound notes will circulate chiefly among little shopkeepers, butchers, bakers, market-people, renters of small houses, lodgers, etc. All the high departments of commerce and the affluent stations of life were already *overstocked*, as Smith expresses it, with the bank notes. No place remained open wherein to crowd an additional quantity of bank notes but among the class of people I have just mentioned, and the means of doing this could be best effected by coining five-pound notes. This conduct has the appearance of that of an unprincipled insolvent, who, when on the verge of bankruptcy to the amount of many thousands, will borrow as low as five pounds of the servants in his house, and break the next day.

[23] Part of the inscription on an English guinea.

But whatever momentary relief or aid the minister and his bank might expect from this low contrivance of five-pound notes, it will increase the inability of the bank to pay the higher notes, and hasten the destruction of all; for even the small taxes that used to be paid in money will now be paid in those notes, and the bank will soon find itself with scarcely any other money than what the hair-powder guinea-tax brings in.

The bank notes make the most serious part of the business of finance: what is called the national funded debt is but a trifle when put in comparison with it; yet the case of the bank notes has never been touched upon. But it certainly ought to be known upon what authority, whether that of the minister or of the directors, and upon what foundation, such immense quantities are issued. I have stated the amount of them at sixty millions; I have produced data for that estimation; and besides this, the apparent quantity of them, far beyond that of gold and silver in the nation, corroborates the statement. But were there but a third part of sixty millions, the bank cannot pay half a crown in the pound; for no new supply of money, as before said, can arrive at the bank, as all the taxes will be paid in paper.

When the funding system began, it was not doubted that the loans that had been borrowed would be repaid. Government not only propagated that belief, but it began paying them off. In time this profession came to be abandoned: and it is not difficult to see that bank notes will march the same way; for the amount of them is only another debt under another name; and the probability is that Mr. Pitt will at last propose funding them. In that case bank notes will not be so valuable as French assignats. The assignats have a solid property in reserve, in the national domains; bank notes have none; and, besides this, the English revenue must then sink down to what the amount of it was before the funding system began—between three and four millions; one of which the *arch-treasurer* would require for himself, and the arch-treasurer *apparent* would require three-quarters of a million more to pay his debts. "In France," says Sterne, "they order these things better."

I have now exposed the English system of finance to the eyes of all nations; for this work will be published in all languages. In doing this, I have done an act of justice to those numerous citizens of neutral nations who have been imposed upon by that fraudulent system, and who have property at stake upon the event.

As an individual citizen of America, and as far as an individual can go, I have revenged (if I may use the expression without any immoral meaning) the piratical depredations committed on the American commerce by the English government. I have retaliated for France on the subject of finance: and I conclude with retorting on Mr. Pitt the expression he used against France, and say, that the English system of finance "IS ON THE VERGE, NAY EVEN IN THE GULF OF BANKRUPTCY."

THOMAS PAINE.

Paris, 19th Germinal. 4th year of the Republic, April 8, 1796.

AGRARIAN JUSTICE

Editor's Introduction

This pamphlet appeared first in Paris, 1797, with the title: "Thomas Payne à La Législature et au Directoire. Ou la Justice Agraire opposée à la Loi Agraire, et aux privilèges agraires. Prix 15 sols. À Paris, chez la citoyenne Ragouleau, près le Théâtre de la République, No. 229. Et chez les Marchands de Nouveautés." A prefatory note says (translated): "The sudden departure of Thomas Paine has prevented his supervising the translation of this work, to which he attached great value. He entrusted it to a friend. It is for the reader to decide whether the scheme here set forth is worthy of the publicity given it." (Paine had gone to Havre early in May with the Monroes, intending to accompany them to America, but, rightly suspecting plans for his capture by an English cruiser, returned to Paris.) In the same year the pamphlet was printed in English, by W. Adlard in Paris, and in London for "T. Williams, No. 8 Little Turnstile, Holborn." Paine's preface to the London edition contained some sentences which the publishers, as will be seen, suppressed under asterisks, and two sentences were omitted from the pamphlet which I have supplied from the French. The English title adds a brief resumé of Paine's scheme to the caption—"Agrarian Justice opposed to Agrarian Law, and to Agrarian Monopoly." The work was written in the winter of 1795–6, when Paine was still an invalid in Monroe's house, though not published until 1797.

The prefatory Letter to the Legislature and the Directory, now for the first time printed in English, is of much historical interest, and shows the title of the pamphlet related to the rise of Socialism in France. The leader of that movement, François Noel Babeuf, a frantic and pathetic figure of the time, had just been executed. He had named himself "Gracchus," and called his journal *Tribune du Peuple*, in homage to the Roman Tribune, Caius Gracchus, the original socialist and agrarian, whose fate (suicide of himself and his servant) Babeuf and his disciple Darthé invoked in prison, whence they were carried bleeding to the guillotine. This, however, was on account of the conspiracy they had formed, with the remains of the Robespierrian party and some disguised royalists, to overthrow the government. The socialistic propaganda of Babeuf, however, prevailed over all other elements of the conspiracy: the reactionary features of the Constitution, especially the property qualification of suffrage of whose effects Paine had warned the Convention in his speech on July 7th, 1795, and the poverty which survived a revolution that promised its abolition, had excited wide discontent. The "Babouvists" numbered as many as 17,000 in Paris. Babeuf and Lepelletier were appointed by the secret council of this fraternity (which took the name of "Equals") a "Directory of Public Safety." May 11, 1796, was fixed for seizing on the government, and Babeuf had prepared his Proclamation of the socialistic millennium. But the plot was discovered, May 10th, the leaders arrested, and, after a year's delay, two of them executed—the best-hearted men in the movement, Babeuf and Darthé.

Paine too had been moved by the cry for "Bread, and the Constitution of '93"; and it is a notable coincidence that in that winter of 1795–6, while the socialists were secretly plotting to seize the kingdom of heaven by violence, Paine was devising his plan of relief by taxing inheritances of land, anticipating by a hundred years the English budget of Sir William Harcourt. Babeuf having failed in his socialist, and Pichegru in his royalist, plot, their blows were yet fatal: there still remained in the hearts of millions a Babeuf or a Pichegru awaiting the chieftain strong enough to combine them, as Napoleon presently did, making all the nation "Égaux" as parts of a mighty military engine, and satisfying the royalist triflers with the pomp and glory of war.

Author's Inscription

To the Legislature and the Executive Directory of the French Republic

The plan contained in this work is not adapted for any particular country alone: the principle on which it is based is general. But as the rights of man are a new study in this world, and one needing protection from priestly imposture, and the insolence of oppressions too long established, I have thought it right to place this little work under your safeguard. When we reflect on the long and dense night in which France and all Europe have remained plunged by their governments and their priests, we must feel less surprise than grief at the bewilderment caused by the first burst of light that dispels the darkness. The eye accustomed to darkness can hardly bear at first the broad daylight. It is by usage the eye learns to see, and it is the same in passing from any situation to its opposite.

As we have not at one instant renounced all our errors, we cannot at one stroke acquire knowledge of all our rights. France has had the honour of adding to the word *Liberty* that of *Equality*; and this word signifies essentially a principal that admits of no gradation in the things to which it applies. But equality is often misunderstood, often misapplied, and often violated.

Liberty and *Property* are words expressing all those of our possessions which are not of an intellectual nature. There are two kinds of property. Firstly, natural property, or that which comes to us from the Creator of the universe—such as the earth, air, water. Secondly, artificial or acquired property—the invention of men. In the latter equality is impossible; for to distribute it equally it would be necessary that all should have contributed in the same proportion, which can never be the case; and this being the case, every individual would hold on to his own property, as his right share. Equality of natural property is the subject of this little essay. Every individual in the world is born therein with legitimate claims on a certain kind of property, or its equivalent.

The right of voting for persons charged with the execution of the laws that govern society is inherent in the word Liberty, and constitutes the equality of personal rights. But even if that right (of voting) were inherent in property, which I deny, the right of suffrage would still belong to all equally, because, as I have said, all individuals have legitimate birthrights in a certain species of property.

I have always considered the present Constitution of the French Republic the *best organized system* the human mind has yet produced. But I hope my former colleagues will not be offended if I warn them of an error which has slipped into its principle. Equality of the right of suffrage is not maintained. This right is in it connected with a condition on which it ought not to depend; that is, with a proportion of a certain tax called "direct." The dignity of suffrage is thus lowered; and, in placing it in the scale with an inferior thing, the enthusiasm that right is capable of inspiring is diminished. It is impossible to find any equivalent counterpoise for the right of suffrage, because it is alone worthy to be its own basis, and cannot thrive as a graft, or an appendage.

Since the Constitution was established we have seen two conspiracies stranded—that of Babeuf, and that of some obscure personages who decorate themselves with the despicable name of "royalists." The defect in principle of the Constitution was the origin of Babeuf's conspiracy. He availed himself of the resentment caused by this flaw, and instead of seeking a remedy by legitimate and constitutional means, or proposing some measure useful to society, the conspirators did their best to renew disorder and confusion, and constituted themselves personally into a Directory, which is formally destructive of election and representation. They were, in fine, extravagant enough to suppose that society, occupied with its domestic affairs, would blindly yield to them a directorship usurped by violence.

The conspiracy of Babeuf was followed in a few months by that of the royalists, who foolishly flattered themselves with the notion of doing great things by feeble or foul means. They counted on all the discontented, from whatever cause, and tried to rouse, in their turn, the class of people who had been following the others. But these new chiefs acted as if they thought society had nothing more at heart than to maintain courtiers, pensioners, and all their train, under the contemptible title of royalty. My little essay will disabuse them, by showing that society is aiming at a very different end—maintaining itself.

We all know or should know, that the time during which a revolution is proceeding is not the time when its resulting advantages can be enjoyed. But had Babeuf and his accomplices taken into consideration the condition of France under this constitution, and compared it with what it was under the tragical revolutionary government, and during the execrable reign of Terror, the rapidity of the alteration must have appeared to them very striking and astonishing. Famine has been replaced by abundance, and by the well-founded hope of a near and increasing prosperity.

As for the defect in the Constitution, I am fully convinced that it will be rectified constitutionally, and that this step is indispensable; for so long as it continues it will inspire the hopes and furnish the means of conspirators; and for the rest, it is regrettable that a Constitution so wisely organized should err so much in its principle. This fault exposes it to other dangers which will make themselves felt. Intriguing candidates will go about among those who have not the means to pay the direct tax and pay it for them, on condition of receiving their votes. Let us maintain inviolably equality in the sacred right of suffrage: public security can never have a basis more solid. *Salut et Fraternité.*

Your former colleague,
THOMAS PAINE.

Author's English Preface

The following little Piece was written in the winter of 1795 and 96; and, as I had not determined whether to publish it during the present war, or to wait till the commencement of a peace, it has lain by me, without alteration or addition, from the time it was written.

What has determined me to publish it now is, a sermon preached by Watson, Bishop of Llandaff. Some of my Readers will recollect, that this Bishop wrote a Book entitled *An Apology for the Bible* in answer to my Second Part of the *Age of Reason*. I procured a copy of his Book, and he may depend upon hearing from me on that subject.

At the end of the Bishop's Book is a List of the Works he has written. Among which is the sermon alluded to; it is entitled: "The Wisdom and Goodness of God, in Having Made Both Rich and Poor; with an Appendix, Containing Reflections on the Present State of England and France."

The error contained in this sermon determined me to publish my Agrarian Justice. It is wrong to say God made *rich and poor*; he made only *male and female*; and he gave them the earth for their inheritance....[24]

Instead of preaching to encourage one part of mankind in insolence... it would be better that Priests employed their time to render the general condition of man less miserable than it is. Practical religion consists in doing good: and the only way of serving God is, that of endeavouring to make his creation happy. All preaching that has not this for its object is nonsense and hypocracy.

[24] The omissions are noted in the English edition of 1797. —Conway

Agrarian Justice

To preserve the benefits of what is called civilized life, and to remedy at the same time the evil which it has produced, ought to be considered as one of the first objects of reformed legislation.

Whether that state that is proudly, perhaps erroneously, called civilization, has most promoted or most injured the general happiness of man, is a question that may be strongly contested. On one side, the spectator is dazzled by splendid appearances; on the other, he is shocked by extremes of wretchedness; both of which it has erected. The most affluent and the most miserable of the human race are to be found in the countries that are called civilized.

To understand what the state of society ought to be, it is necessary to have some idea of the natural and primitive state of man; such as it is at this day among the Indians of North America. There is not, in that state, any of those spectacles of human misery which poverty and want present to our eyes in all the towns and streets in Europe. Poverty, therefore, is a thing created by that which is called civilized life. It exists not in the natural state. On the other hand, the natural state is without those advantages which flow from agriculture, arts, science, and manufactures.

The life of an Indian is a continual holiday, compared with the poor of Europe; and, on the other hand it appears to be abject when compared to the rich. Civilization, therefore, or that which is so called, has operated two ways: to make one part of society more affluent, and the other more wretched, than would have been the lot of either in a natural state.

It is always possible to go from the natural to the civilized state, but it is never possible to go from the civilized to the natural state. The reason is, that man in a natural state, subsisting by hunting, requires ten times the quantity of land to range over to procure himself sustenance, than would support him in a civilized state, where the earth is cultivated. When, therefore, a country becomes populous by the additional aids of cultivation, art, and science, there is a necessity of preserving things in that state; because without it there cannot be sustenance for more, perhaps, than a tenth part of its inhabitants. The thing, therefore, now to be done is to remedy the evils and preserve the benefits that have arisen to society by passing from the natural to that which is called the civilized state.

In taking the matter upon this ground, the first principle of civilization ought to have been, and ought still to be, that the condition of every person born into the world, after a state of civilization commences, ought not to be worse than if he had been born before that period. But the fact is, that the condition of millions, in every country in Europe, is far worse than if they had been born before civilization began, or had been born among the Indians of North America at the present day. I will show how this fact has happened.

It is a position not to be controverted that the earth, in its natural uncultivated state was, and ever would have continued to be, *the common property of the human race*. In that state every man would have been born to property. He would have been a joint life proprietor with the rest in the property of the soil, and in all its natural productions, vegetable and animal.

But the earth in its natural state, as before said, is capable of supporting but a small number of inhabitants compared with what it is capable of doing in a cultivated state. And as it is impossible to separate the improvement made by cultivation from the earth itself, upon which that improvement is made, the idea of landed property arose from that inseparable connection; but it is nevertheless true, that it is the value of the improvement only, and not the earth itself, that is individual property. Every proprietor, therefore, of cultivated land, owes to the community a *ground-rent* (for I know of no better term to express the idea) for the land which he holds; and it is from this ground-rent that the fund proposed in this plan is to issue.

It is deducible, as well from the nature of the thing as from all the histories transmitted to us, that the idea of landed property commenced with cultivation, and that there was no such thing as landed property before that time. It could not exist in the first state of man, that of hunters. It did not exist in the second state, that of shepherds: neither Abraham,

Isaac, Jacob, nor Job, so far as the history of the Bible may be credited in probable things, were owners of land. Their property consisted, as is always enumerated, in flocks and herds, and they travelled with them from place to place. The frequent contentions at that time, about the use of a well in the dry country of Arabia, where those people lived, also show that there was no landed property. It was not admitted that land could be claimed as property.

There could be no such thing as landed property originally. Man did not make the earth, and, though he had a natural right to occupy it, he had no right to locate as his property in perpetuity any part of it; neither did the creator of the earth open a land-office, from whence the first title-deeds should issue. Whence then, arose the idea of landed property? I answer as before, that when cultivation began the idea of landed property began with it, from the impossibility of separating the improvement made by cultivation from the earth itself, upon which that improvement was made. The value of the improvement so far exceeded the value of the natural earth, at that time, as to absorb it; till, in the end, the common right of all became confounded into the cultivated right of the individual. But there are, nevertheless, distinct species of rights, and will continue to be so long as the earth endures.

It is only by tracing things to their origin that we can gain rightful ideas of them, and it is by gaining such ideas that we discover the boundary that divides right from wrong, and teaches every man to know his own. I have entitled this tract Agrarian Justice, to distinguish it from Agrarian Law. Nothing could be more unjust than Agrarian Law in a country improved by cultivation; for though every man, as an inhabitant of the earth, is a joint proprietor of it in its natural state, it does not follow that he is a joint proprietor of cultivated earth. The additional value made by cultivation, after the system was admitted, became the property of those who did it, or who inherited it from them, or who purchased it. It had originally no owner. Whilst, therefore, I advocate the right, and interest myself in the hard case of all those who have been thrown out of their natural inheritance by the introduction of the system of landed property, I equally defend the right of the possessor to the part which is his.

Cultivation is at least one of the greatest natural improvements ever made by human invention. It has given to created earth a tenfold value. But the landed monopoly that began with it has produced the greatest evil. It has dispossessed more than half the inhabitants of every nation of their natural inheritance, without providing for them, as ought to have been done, an indemnification for that loss, and has thereby created a species of poverty and wretchedness that did not exist before.

In advocating the case of the persons thus dispossessed, it is a right, and not a charity, that I am pleading for. But it is that kind of right which, being neglected at first, could not be brought forward afterwards till heaven had opened the way by a revolution in the system of government. Let us then do honour to revolutions by justice, and give currency to their principles by blessings.

Having thus in a few words, opened the merits of the case, I shall now proceed to the plan I have to propose, which is,

To create a National Fund, out of which there shall be paid to every person, when arrived at the age of twenty-one years, the sum of fifteen pounds sterling, as a compensation in part, for the loss of his or her natural inheritance, by the introduction of the system of landed property:

And also, the sum of ten pounds per annum, during life, to every person now living, of the age of fifty years, and to all others as they shall arrive at that age.

MEANS BY WHICH THE FUND IS TO BE CREATED

I have already established the principle, namely, that the earth, in its natural uncultivated state was, and ever would have continued to be, the *common property of the human race*; that in that state, every person would have been born to property; and that the system of landed property, by its inseparable connection with cultivation, and with what is called civilized life, has absorbed the property of all those whom it dispossessed, without providing, as ought to have been done, an indemnification for that loss.

The fault, however, is not in the present possessors. No complaint is intended, or ought to be alleged against them, unless they adopt the crime by opposing justice. The fault is in the system, and it has stolen imperceptibly upon the world, aided afterwards by the agrarian law of the sword. But the fault can be made to reform itself by successive generations; and without diminishing or deranging the property of any of the present possessors, the operation of the fund can yet commence, and be in full activity, the first year of its establishment, or soon after, as I shall show.

It is proposed that the payments, as already stated, be made to every person, rich or poor. It is best to make it so, to prevent invidious distinctions. It is also right it should be so, because it is in lieu of the natural inheritance, which, as a right, belongs to every man, over and above the property he may have created, or inherited from those who did. Such persons as do not choose to receive it can throw it into the common fund.

Taking it then for granted that no person ought to be in a worse condition when born under what is called a state of civilization, than he would have been had he been born in a state of nature, and that civilization ought to have made, and ought still to make, provision for that purpose, it can only be done by subtracting from property a portion equal in value to the natural inheritance it has absorbed.

Various methods may be proposed for this purpose, but that which appears to be the best (not only because it will operate without deranging any present possessors, or without interfering with the collection of taxes or *emprunts* necessary for the purposes of government and the revolution, but because it will be the least troublesome and the most effectual, and also because the subtraction will be made at a time that best admits it) is at the moment that property is passing by the death of one person to the possession of another. In this case, the bequeather gives nothing: the receiver pays nothing. The only matter to him is, that the monopoly of natural inheritance, to which there never was a right, begins to cease in his person. A generous man would not wish it to continue, and a just man will rejoice to see it abolished.

My state of health prevents my making sufficient inquiries with respect to the doctrine of probabilities, whereon to found calculations with such degrees of certainty as they are capable of. What, therefore, I offer on this head is more the result of observation and reflection than of received information; but I believe it will be found to agree sufficiently with fact.

In the first place, taking twenty-one years as the epoch of maturity, all the property of a nation, real and personal, is always in the possession of persons above that age. It is then necessary to know, as a datum of calculation, the average of years which persons above that age will live. I take this average to be about thirty years, for though many persons will live forty, fifty, or sixty years after the age of twenty-one years, others will die much sooner, and some in every year of that time.

Taking, then, thirty years as the average of time, it will give, without any material variation one way or other, the average of time in which the whole property or capital of a nation, or a sum equal thereto, will have passed through one entire revolution in descent, that is, will have gone by deaths to new possessors; for though, in many instances, some parts of this capital will remain forty, fifty, or sixty years in the possession of one person, other parts will have revolved two or three times before those thirty years expire, which will bring it to that average; for were one half the capital of a nation to revolve twice in thirty years, it would produce the same fund as if the whole revolved once.

Taking, then, thirty years as the average of time in which the whole capital of a nation, or a sum equal thereto, will revolve once, the thirtieth part thereof will be the sum that will revolve every year, that is, will go by deaths to new possessors; and this last sum being thus known, and the ratio percent to be subtracted from it determined, it will give the annual amount or income of the proposed fund, to be applied as already mentioned.

In looking over the discourse of the English minister, Pitt, in his opening of what is called in England the budget, (the scheme of finance for the year 1796,) I find an estimate of the national capital of that country. As this estimate of a national capital is prepared ready to my hand, I take it as a datum to act upon. When a calculation is made upon the known capital of any nation, combined with its population, it will serve as a scale for any other nation, in proportion as its capital and population be more or less. I am the more disposed to take this estimate of Mr. Pitt, for the purpose of showing to that minister, upon his own calculation, how much better money may be employed than in wasting it, as he has done, on the wild project of setting up Bourbon kings. What, in the name of heaven, are Bourbon kings to the people of England? It is better that the people have bread.

Mr. Pitt states the national capital of England, real and personal, to be one thousand three hundred millions sterling, which is about one-fourth part of the national capital of France, including Belgia. The event of the last harvest in each country proves that the soil of France is more productive than that of England, and that it can better support twenty-four or twenty-five millions of inhabitants than that of England can seven or seven and a half millions.

The thirtieth part of this capital of £1,300,000,000 is £43,333,333 which is the part that will revolve every year by deaths in that country to new possessors; and the sum that will annually revolve in France in the proportion of four to one, will be about one hundred and seventy-three millions sterling. From this sum of £43,333,333 annually revolving, is to be subtracted the value of the natural inheritance absorbed in it, which, perhaps, in fair justice, cannot be taken at less, and ought not to be taken for more, than a tenth part.

It will always happen, that of the property thus revolving by deaths every year a part will descend in a direct line to sons and daughters, and the other part collaterally, and the proportion will be found to be about three to one; that is, about thirty millions of the above sum will descend to direct heirs, and the remaining sum of £13,333,333 to more distant relations, and in part to strangers.

Considering, then, that man is always related to society, that relationship will become comparatively greater in proportion as the next of kin is more distant, it is therefore consistent with civilization to say that where there are no direct heirs society shall be heir to a part over and above the tenth part *due* to society. If this additional part be from five to ten or twelve percent, in proportion as the next of kin be nearer or more remote, so as to average with the escheats that may fall, which ought always to go to society and not to the government (an addition of ten percent more), the produce from the annual sum of £43,333,333 will be:

From	£30,000,000	at ten percent.	£3,000,000
From	£13,333,333	at ten percent with the addition of ten percent more.	£2,666,666
	£43,333,333		£5,666,666

Having thus arrived at the annual amount of the proposed fund, I come, in the next place, to speak of the population proportioned to this fund, and to compare it with the uses to which the fund is to be applied.

The population (I mean that of England) does not exceed seven millions and a half, and the number of persons above the age of fifty will in that case be about four hundred thousand. There would not, however, be more than that number that would accept the proposed ten pounds sterling per annum, though they would be entitled to it. I have no idea it would be accepted by many persons who had a yearly income of two or three hundred pounds sterling. But as we often see instances of rich people falling into sudden poverty, even at the age of sixty, they would always have the right of drawing all the arrears due to them. Four millions, therefore, of the above annual sum of £5,666,666 will be required for four hundred thousand aged persons, at ten pounds sterling each.

I come now to speak of the persons annually arriving at twenty-one years of age. If all the persons who died were above the age of twenty-one years, the number of persons annually arriving at that age, must be equal to the annual number of deaths, to keep the population stationary. But the greater part die under the age of twenty-one, and therefore the number of persons annually arriving at twenty-one will be less than half the number of deaths. The whole number of deaths upon a population of seven millions and an half will be about 220,000 annually. The number arriving at twenty-one years of age will be about 100,000. The whole number of these will not receive the proposed fifteen pounds, for the reasons already mentioned, though, as in the former case, they would be entitled to it. Admitting then that a tenth part declined receiving it, the amount would stand thus:

Scope	*Subtotal*	*Total*
Fund annually		£5,666,666
To 400,000 aged persons at £10 each	£4,000,000	
To 90,000 persons of 21 years, £15 ster. each	£1,350,000	
		£5,350,000
	Remains	£316,666

There are, in every country, a number of blind and lame persons, totally incapable of earning a livelihood. But as it will always happen that the greater number of blind persons will be among those who are above the age of fifty years, they will be provided for in that class. The remaining sum of £316,666 will provide for the lame and blind under that age, at the same rate of £10 annually for each person.

Having now gone through all the necessary calculations, and stated the particulars of the plan, I shall conclude with some observations.

It is not charity but a right, not bounty but justice, that I am pleading for. The present state of civilization is as odious as it is unjust. It is absolutely the opposite of what it should be, and it is necessary that a revolution should be made in it.[25] The contrast of affluence and

[25] This and the preceding sentence are omitted in all previous English and American editions. —Conway

wretchedness continually meeting and offending the eye, is like dead and living bodies chained together. Though I care as little about riches, as any man, I am a friend to riches because they are capable of good. I care not how affluent some may be, provided that none be miserable in consequence of it. But it is impossible to enjoy affluence with the felicity it is capable of being enjoyed, whilst so much misery is mingled in the scene. The sight of the misery, and the unpleasant sensations it suggests, which, though they may be suffocated cannot be extinguished, are a greater drawback upon the felicity of affluence than the proposed ten percent upon property is worth. He that would not give the one to get rid of the other has no charity, even for himself.

There are, in every country, some magnificent charities established by individuals. It is, however, but little that any individual can do, when the whole extent of the misery to be relieved is considered. He may satisfy his conscience, but not his heart. He may give all that he has, and that all will relieve but little. It is only by organizing civilization upon such principles as to act like a system of pullies, that the whole weight of misery can be removed.

The plan here proposed will reach the whole. It will immediately relieve and take out of view three classes of wretchedness—the blind, the lame, and the aged poor; and it will furnish the rising generation with means to prevent their becoming poor; and it will do this without deranging or interfering with any national measures. To show that this will be the case, it is sufficient to observe that the operation and effect of the plan will, in all cases, be the same as if every individual were *voluntarily* to make his will and dispose of his property in the manner here proposed.

But it is justice, and not charity, that is the principle of the plan. In all great cases it is necessary to have a principle more universally active than charity; and, with respect to justice, it ought not to be left to the choice of detached individuals whether they will do justice or not. Considering then, the plan on the ground of justice, it ought to be the act of the whole, growing spontaneously out of the principles of the revolution, and the reputation of it ought to be national and not individual.

A plan upon this principle would benefit the revolution by the energy that springs from the consciousness of justice. It would multiply also the national resources; for property, like vegetation, increases by offsets. When a young couple begin the world, the difference is exceedingly great whether they begin with nothing or with fifteen pounds apiece. With this aid they could buy a cow, and implements to cultivate a few acres of land; and instead of becoming burdens upon society, which is always the case where children are produced faster than they can be fed, would be put in the way of becoming useful and profitable citizens. The national domains also would sell the better if pecuniary aids were provided to cultivate them in small lots.

It is the practice of what has unjustly obtained the name of civilization (and the practice merits not to be called either charity or policy) to make some provision for persons becoming poor and wretched only at the time they become so. Would it not, even as a matter of economy, be far better to adopt means to prevent their becoming poor? This can best be done by making every person when arrived at the age of twenty-one years an inheritor of something to begin with. The rugged face of society, chequered with the extremes of affluence and want, proves that some extraordinary violence has been committed upon it, and calls on justice for redress. The great mass of the poor in all countries are become an hereditary race, and it is next to impossible for them to get cut of that state of themselves. It ought also to be observed that this mass increases in all countries that are called civilized. More persons fall annually into it than get out of it.

Though in a plan of which justice and humanity are the foundation-principles, interest ought not to be admitted into the calculation, yet it is always of advantage to the establishment of any plan to show that it is beneficial as a matter of interest. The success of any proposed plan submitted to public consideration must finally depend on the numbers interested in supporting it, united with the justice of its principles.

The plan here proposed will benefit all, without injuring any. It will consolidate the interest of the Republic with that of the individual. To the numerous class dispossessed of their natural inheritance by the system of landed property it will be an act of national justice. To persons dying possessed of moderate fortunes it will operate as a tontine to their children, more beneficial than the sum of money paid into the fund: and it will give to the accumulation of riches a degree of security that none of the old governments of Europe, now tottering on their foundations, can give.

I do not suppose that more than one family in ten, in any of the countries of Europe, has, when the head of the family dies, a clear property left of five hundred pounds sterling. To all such the plan is advantageous. That property would pay fifty pounds into the fund, and if there were only two children under age they would receive fifteen pounds each, (thirty pounds,) on coming of age, and be entitled to ten pounds a-year after fifty. It is from the overgrown acquisition of property that the fund will support itself; and I know that the possessors of such property in England, though they would eventually be benefited by the protection of nine-tenths of it, will exclaim against the plan. But without entering into any inquiry how they came by that property, let them recollect that they have been the advocates of this war, and that Mr. Pitt has already laid on more new taxes to be raised annually upon the people of England, and that for supporting the despotism of Austria and the Bourbons against the liberties of France, than would pay annually all the sums proposed in this plan.

I have made the calculations stated in this plan, upon what is called personal, as well as upon landed property. The reason for making it upon land is already explained; and the reason for taking personal property into the calculation is equally well founded though on a different principle. Land, as before said, is the free gift of the Creator in common to the human race. Personal property is the effect of society; and it is as impossible for an individual to acquire personal property without the aid of society, as it is for him to make land originally. Separate an individual from society, and give him an island or a continent to possess, and he cannot acquire personal property. He cannot be rich. So inseparably are the means connected with the end, in all cases, that where the former do not exist the latter cannot be obtained. All accumulation, therefore, of personal property, beyond what a man's own hands produce, is derived to him by living in society; and he owes on every principle of justice, of gratitude, and of civilization, a part of that accumulation back again to society from whence the whole came. This is putting the matter on a general principle, and perhaps it is best to do so; for if we examine the case minutely it will be found that the accumulation of personal property is, in many instances, the effect of paying too little for the labour that produced it; the consequence of which is, that the working hand perishes in old age, and the employer abounds in affluence. It is, perhaps, impossible to proportion exactly the price of labour to the profits it produces; and it will also be said, as an apology for the injustice, that were a workman to receive an increase of wages daily he would not save it against old age, nor be much better for it in the interim. Make, then, society the treasurer to guard it for him in a common fund; for it is no reason, that because he might not make a good use of it for himself, another should take it.

The state of civilization that has prevailed throughout Europe, is as unjust in its principle, as it is horrid in its effects; and it is the consciousness of this, and the apprehension that such a state cannot continue when once investigation begins in any country, that makes the possessors of property dread every idea of a revolution. It is the hazard and not the principle of revolutions that retards their progress. This being the case, it is necessary as well for the protection of property, as for the sake of justice and humanity, to form a system that, whilst it preserves one part of society from wretchedness, shall secure the other from depredation.

The superstitious awe, the enslaving reverence, that formerly surrounded affluence, is passing away in all countries, and leaving the possessor of property to the convulsion of accidents. When wealth and splendour, instead of fascinating the multitude, excite emotions of disgust; when, instead of drawing forth admiration, it is beheld as an insult upon wretchedness; when the ostentatious appearance it makes serves to call the right of it in question, the case of property becomes critical, and it is only in a system of justice that the possessor can contemplate security.

To remove the danger, it is necessary to remove the antipathies, and this can only be done by making property productive of a national blessing, extending to every individual. When the riches of one man above another shall increase the national fund in the same proportion; when it shall be seen that the prosperity of that fund depends on the prosperity of individuals; when the more riches a man acquires, the better it shall be for the general mass; it is then that antipathies will cease, and property be placed on the permanent basis of national interest and protection.

I have no property in France to become subject to the plan I propose. What I have which is not much, is in the United States of America. But I will pay one hundred pounds sterling towards this fund in France, the instant it shall be established; and I will pay the same sum in England whenever a similar establishment shall take place in that country.

A revolution in the state of civilization is the necessary companion of revolutions in the system of government. If a revolution in any country be from bad to good, or from good to bad, the state of what is called civilization in that country, must be made conformable thereto, to give that revolution effect. Despotic government supports itself by abject civilization, in which debasement of the human mind, and wretchedness in the mass of the people, are the chief criterions. Such governments consider man merely as an animal; that the exercise of intellectual faculty is not his privilege; *that he has nothing to do with the laws but to obey them*;[26] and they politically depend more upon breaking the spirit of the people by poverty, than they fear enraging it by desperation.

It is a revolution in the state of civilization that will give perfection to the revolution of France. Already the conviction that government by representation is the true system of government is spreading itself fast in the world. The reasonableness of it can be seen by all. The justness of it makes itself felt even by its opposers. But when a system of civilization, growing out of that system of government, shall be so organized that not a man or woman born in the Republic but shall inherit some means of beginning the world, and see before them the certainty of escaping the miseries that under other governments accompany old age, the revolution of France will have an advocate and an ally in the heart of all nations.

An army of principles will penetrate where an army of soldiers cannot; it will succeed where diplomatic management would fail: it is neither the Rhine, the Channel, nor the Ocean that can arrest its progress: it will march on the horizon of the world, and it will conquer.

MEANS FOR CARRYING THE PROPOSED PLAN INTO EXECUTION, AND TO RENDER IT AT THE SAME TIME CONDUCIVE TO THE PUBLIC INTEREST

I. Each canton shall elect in its primary assemblies, three persons, as commissioners for that canton, who shall take cognizance, and keep a register of all matters happening in that canton, conformable to the charter that shall be established by law for carrying this plan into execution.

II. The law shall fix the manner in which the property of deceased persons shall be ascertained.

[26] Expression of Horsley, an English bishop, in the English parliament.

III. When the amount of the property of any deceased person shall be ascertained, the principal heir to that property, or the eldest of the co-heirs, if of lawful age, or if under age the person authorized by the will of the deceased to represent him or them, shall give bond to the commissioners of the canton to pay the said tenth part thereof in four equal quarterly payments, within the space of one year or sooner, at the choice of the payers. One half of the whole property shall remain as a security until the bond be paid off.

IV. The bond shall be registered in the office of the commissioners of the canton, and the original bonds shall be deposited in the national bank at Paris. The bank shall publish every quarter of a year the amount of the bonds in its possession, and also the bonds that shall have been paid off, or what parts thereof, since the last quarterly publication.

V. The national bank shall issue bank notes upon the security of the bonds in its possession. The notes so issued, shall be applied to pay the pensions of aged persons, and the compensations to persons arriving at twenty-one years of age. It is both reasonable and generous to suppose, that persons not under immediate necessity, will suspend their right of drawing on the fund, until it acquire, as it will do, a greater degree of ability. In this case, it is proposed, that an honorary register be kept, in each canton, of the names of the persons thus suspending that right, at least during the present war.

VI. As the inheritors of property must always take up their bonds in four quarterly payments, or sooner if they choose, there will always be *numéraire* [cash] arriving at the bank after the expiration of the first quarter, to exchange for the bank notes that shall be brought in.

VII. The bank notes being thus put in circulation, upon the best of all possible security, that of actual property, to more than four times the amount of the bonds upon which the notes are issued, and with *numéraire* continually arriving at the bank to exchange or pay them off whenever they shall be presented for that purpose, they will acquire a permanent value in all parts of the Republic. They can therefore be received in payment of taxes, or *emprunts* equal to *numéraire*, because the government can always receive *numéraire* for them at the bank.

VIII. It will be necessary that the payments of the ten percent be made in *numéraire* for the first year from the establishment of the plan. But after the expiration of the first year, the inheritors of property may pay ten percent either in bank notes issued upon the fund, or in *numéraire*, If the payments be in *numéraire*, it will lie as a deposit at the bank, to be exchanged for a quantity of notes equal to that amount; and if in notes issued upon the fund, it will cause a demand upon the fund, equal thereto; and thus the operation of the plan will create means to carry itself into execution.

THOMAS PAINE.